WANT TO LEARN MORE?

If after reading this book, you would like to learn more about topics we discussed, please visit our frequently updated blog section:

Centivis.com/news

You can download free reports on diagnostics reimbursement pathways, country periodic tariff changes and diagnostic test reports:

Centivis.com/insights

Or just simply sign up to the mailing list to receive our monthly newsletter delivered in your inbox:

Centivis.com

DIAGNOSTICS
REIMBURSEMENT
COMPASS

A 90-Minute Guide to
Define, Demonstrate and Capture
Diagnostics Value Confidently

NORBERT FARKAS

To Nicole and Julia:

Never stop exploring.

Published by:
Centivis AG
Suurstoffi 37. 6343
Rotkreuz, Switzerland

020321

Disclaimer:

This book contains the opinions and ideas of the author. The material in this book is provided for informational purposes only and is not intended to be, and should not be interpreted as, specific reimbursement or billing advice.

Although the author and publisher have made every effort to ensure the information in this book was correct at press time, the author and the publisher do not assume and hereby disclaim any liability to any party for any loss, danger, or disruption caused by errors or omissions, whether such errors or omissions results from negligence accident or any other cause.

The advice, examples and strategies contained herein are not suitable for every situation. The materials contained herein are not intended to represent or guarantee you will achieve the desired results, and the publisher and author make no such guarantee. Neither the publisher nor the author shall be liable for damages arising therefrom.

CONTENTS

FOREWORD

It is not just since the pandemic that we have realized how important diagnostics are for our health and our health systems. Diagnostics allow us to characterize our risk for disease and its complications, identify when we have contracted a disease, guide the selection of appropriate treatments, and allow us to monitor treatment outcomes. While diagnostics do not have a direct health benefit, they help us to manage our risk and avoid certain exposures so that we do not fall ill, and they ensure timely use of the right therapy when this is required.

Diagnostics come in many different flavors, from simple assays like glucose strips to complex molecular procedures (comprehensive genomic profiling, liquid biopsies, noninvasive prenatal testing) and risk algorithms. Some of these diagnostic tests are commoditized, and others are based on cutting edge scientific and digital innovation. Broad access to these diagnostics requires that laboratories include this in their services and are reimbursed by public and private payers. The landscape is much more complex than for pharmaceuticals, where strict processes have been defined for health technology assessment, pricing, and reimbursement. And they are evolving rapidly as we transition towards more complex technologies, including digital apps and biomarkers with their accelerated product life cycles. But very similar to biopharmaceuticals, the goal is to base coverage and pricing decisions on solid scientific evidence, to use our limited health care budgets in the most efficient way, and to ensure that all people can benefit from diagnostic innovation independent of their economic means and place of residence.

In *Diagnostics Reimbursement Compass*, Norbert Farkas provides the first systematic discussion of the issues and processes for achieving reimbursement for in-vitro diagnostics. His clear and pragmatic exposition is based on many years of experience in the diagnostics' industry as well as his consulting practice. He covers the major concepts and elucidates key points with practical examples. Every chapter starts with a nice checklist and key takeaways. The book is concise and can be read in a single sitting, and it can be used as a reference when a specific issue arises. The book finishes with interesting insights on how the author has become successful as an access champion for diagnostics.

This book is a must-read for people working in life science industries, whether they are directly working with diagnostics or developing new medicines that address specific patient and disease segments that can be identified with diagnostic technologies. I found reading *Diagnostics Reimbursement Compass* as 60 minutes very well spent.

Dr. Jens Grueger

Affiliate Professor at the University of Washington School of Pharmacy

Director and Partner at BCG & President (2020-2021) of ISPOR

WHO SHOULD READ
THIS BOOK?

This short book is for experts who are working on launches of innovative, in-vitro diagnostics and would like to learn how to achieve reimbursement in a simple framework.

After climbing the corporate ladder in major life sciences companies (pharmaceuticals, vaccines, and diagnostics) and working on multiple product launches from the pricing, reimbursement, and health economics' perspectives, I transitioned to an advisory role.

With increased responsibilities and having addressed various therapy areas in multiple geographic settings, the puzzle pieces started to connect. Being exposed to senior management, delivering university lectures, and advising numerous clients, I needed to tell the story as simply as possible but not simpler.

In this book, I aim to provide a framework on how to confidently navigate the coverage, reimbursement landscape for in-vitro diagnostic solutions, focusing on key guiding principles, and critical success factors.

No matter if you are part of a leading multinational diagnostics or pharmaceutical manufacturer or an aspiring start-up founder, if you develop, launch, and commercialize new, innovative diagnostics products, you will benefit from the book.

Since the product launch process is a complex, interdisciplinary undertaking, requiring input, coordination, alignment from many different experts, if you specialize on market access, pricing, reimbursement, health economics, sales, marketing, business development, regulatory or medical aspects, you will gain valuable insights from this work.

Your geographic location and place of business is not a limitation. The chapters are designed such that they address the coverage, reimbursement topic holistically with a few supportive country-specific examples, mostly from Europe and/or the United States. If you happen to work in a regional, global capacity, dealing with various markets or you oversee a broader spectrum of the launch process, the content might better resonate with you. For readers seeking country-specific insights, you will benefit from the key principles highlighted in this book, but further research might be required to tailor them to your context.

The frameworks cited in this book may provide mental models and guiding principles on how to address a problem holistically. They may also be helpful in distilling the important concepts and explaining them to a nonexpert audience. If you have just started a new position in the above-mentioned roles or you would like to connect the reimbursement aspects with regulatory, medical, and commercial disciplines, the following chapters are for you.

By writing this book, I would like to draw attention to the importance of diagnostic solutions and laboratory professionals in helping physicians and patients making important decisions. There is a long and bumpy road until new diagnostic solutions are being used in routine practice, with several hurdles to overcome, reimbursement being a major one. I hope this overview will help more industry experts, laboratory professionals, physicians, and payers address reimbursement challenges, ultimately contributing to a better patient access in the diagnostics field.

MY PROMISE TO YOU

Working in a big corporation or running a start-up, you are bombarded with information; you have many emails to answer and several meetings to attend.

Your time is precious.

I promise not to waste your time and attention. This book is intentionally short. I want you to be able to read and understand it quickly and easily.

Within the next 60–90 minutes or so, the *Diagnostics Reimbursement Compass* will provide a simple framework, guiding principles and key aspects of navigating the reimbursement hurdles for in-vitro diagnostic solutions.

I will use plain language, avoid business lingo, simplify messages, and share the essentials of what you need to know to be successful on solving diagnostics reimbursement challenges.

Over the course of the next hour or so, I will:

- Explain why diagnostics reimbursement access matters.
- Share what makes diagnostic tests solutions special.
- Introduce key reimbursement pathways and stakeholder groups.
- Show how to demonstrate diagnostics medical & economic value.
- Triangulate the likely reimbursed price.
- Discuss how to negotiate and secure coverage.
- Provide tips on how to be successful at the job.

On behalf of my entire team, I promise, "We help you capture the value of diagnostics."

INTRODUCTION

B eing in life sciences is fascinating. Developing manufacturing, launching, and commercializing complex medical products that help patients to live better lives require many smart minds, enormous financial commitment, and millions of well-coordinated working hours.

Due to the high research and development risk, complex technologies and increasing clinical evidence requirements, the price tag on innovation is increasing. On the other hand, health systems are under enormous financial pressure. Growing populations, chronic diseases, longer life expectancies, and the COVID-19 pandemic, pose the question: Which medical products and services should be covered or reimbursed by health insurances?

In the last 15 years, I have had the privilege to help find answers to this question from the life science industry perspective. I started as an analyst, and it was fascinating to see how various markets reference each other's pharmaceutical prices and how generic drugs make medicines more affordable. Working on the health economic aspects of various vaccines highlighted the significance of solid clinical and economic evidence, the need for complex modeling and health technology assessments leading to reimbursement discussions and negotiations. My part-time MBA helped me to sharpen my perspective on problems from the managerial viewpoint as I headed the global market access department at a leading diagnostics manufacturer in Switzerland.

Having tackled the same principal access challenges in pharmaceuticals, vaccines and lately in-vitro diagnostics, I have realized how different the diagnostics world is (more about that in the next chapter). These 3 life science business models are similar and naturally, different in parts. My experiences in all 3 aspects have allowed me to understand various aspects, connect the dots, and most importantly, distill complexity into key mental models.

In 2018, I left the industry and founded Centivis, a boutique (digital) diagnostics market access and health policy consulting firm, to help our clients in securing diagnostics reimbursement. In our growing number of projects, no matter the geography, technology, or therapy area, we aim to explore 3 fundamental questions:

1. What is the value and potential price of a diagnostic solution?
2. Who will pay for the test and how?
3. What is required to convince them?

I aim to answer those questions in this book. My entire goal is not to provide a detailed guide, but rather, to give you a compass, which helps you to navigate your own terrain confidently. In each chapter, I will highlight:

1. Why is the question relevant, and why is this an issue in diagnostics?
2. What are the key concepts to keep in mind?
3. What are some real-life examples that illustrate the concepts?

The book is designed so that you can read it cover to cover in a single sitting. It offers the opportunity to explore the topic more or just simply reach out to us to continue the conversation.

So now that you have a better idea of why I authored this book, let us explore why diagnostics access matters and how it differs from other life science industries, e.g., pharmaceuticals.

Chapter #1 Overview

1. Diagnostic tests support many high-stake clinical decisions.

2. Tests and technologies are getting more complex (comprehensive genomic profiling, noninvasive prenatal testing, liquid biopsy, risk scores).

3. Digital diagnostic solutions further disrupt the status quo.

4. Clinical evidence requirements are increasing and linked to more stringent regulatory oversight.

5. Diagnostics reimbursement covers test reports and is mostly cost-based and not brand-specific. In many cases, laboratories and medical societies play a large role, and direct manufacturer engagement may be limited.

6. Reimbursement pathways are diverse with complex stakeholder groups involved.

7. Health technology assessments are not yet utilized consistently in the diagnostics field.

Chapter #1 Overview

8. Cost containment for diagnostics is "knocking on the door."

WHY DOES DIAGNOSTICS ACCESS & REIMBURSEMENT MATTER?

In-vitro diagnostics laboratory testing plays a crucial role in medical decision-making. According to Quest Diagnostics™ and Centers for Disease Control and Prevention (CDC), an estimated 70% of all decisions regarding a patient's diagnosis and treatment, hospital admission and discharge are based on laboratory test results (Quest Diagnostics, 2014) (CDC, 2020), and hospitals spend on average of 3%–4% of their net patient revenue on clinical laboratory services (Quest Diagnostics, 2014).

As we gain finer understanding about diseases and medicine becomes more personalized, diagnostic tests are also getting more complex. Here are few examples:

- By analyzing small fragments of DNA circulating in a pregnant woman's blood, noninvasive prenatal testing (NIPT) can determine the risk of a fetus being born with certain genetic abnormalities, e.g., chromosomal disorders, like Down syndrome (trisomy 21, trisomy 18, trisomy 13) (MedlinePlus®, 2020). This test requires only a simple blood draw and allows doctors to decide if more invasive tests are needed to determine genetic abnormalities with a higher certainty.

- Comprehensive genomic profiling (CGP) leverages next generation sequencing (NGS) to enable detection of oncology biomarkers that help to optimize personalized treatment decisions. CGP intends to replace one-at-time, drug and tumor-type specific companion diagnostic tests with simultaneously testing for all types of genomic alterations for a panel of cancer associated genes. (Nesline, 2019).

- Liquid biopsies examine cancer-related material (like DNA) circulating in the blood, and this may be used to help detect cancer at an early stage, plan or monitor treatments (National Cancer Institute, 2020). A liquid biopsy could be a less invasive alternative, especially when tissue biopsy (standard care for diagnosing cancer) is not feasible due to tumors' locations, multiple metastases, or other health conditions (AACC, 2020).

- Risk prediction models or algorithms can be used to estimate the probability of either having (diagnostic model) or developing a particular disease or outcome (prognostic model). These complex mathematical formulas may combine various laboratory test outcomes, vital signs, medical history, genetic data, and information from wearable devices to support medical decisions. Risk scores require extensive clinical validation to link the score results to the suggested outcomes. A popular cancer risk score, Oncotype DX®, for example, predicts on a scale of 0–100 how likely breast cancer is to recur after surgery and the likely benefit of having chemotherapy (Breast Cancer Now, 2020).

With exponentially growing medical data and the resulting information overload, digital diagnostic solutions are emerging as the "glue" to combine data and to support clinical decisions more efficiently. Technology firms and start-ups are collaborating with established life science companies to launch novel solutions in, e.g., holistic diabetes patient management, which tracks patient outcomes and personalizes lifestyle change advice accordingly; atrial fibrillation remote monitoring, which utilizes convenient patches, smart watches or even mobile phones to monitor a patient's heart rate to detect abnormalities.

As medical decisions become more personalized, the need for thorough clinical evaluation is also increasing. To establish an indication for a diagnostic test (valid reason to use the test), it is necessary to demonstrate its benefit by assessing its safety, technical, diagnostic performance, impact on diagnostic thinking, patient management, and clinical outcome in the chosen patient populations.

Policy makers also keep up with these trends. As an example, in 2017, EU passed new rules for marketing an in-vitro diagnostic medical device, also known as In-Vitro Diagnostics Regulations. IVDR in Europe will:

1. Reclassify the diagnostics tests according to their risk.

2. Require more rigorous clinical evidence and more stringent documentation according to the test's assigned risk class.

3. Increase the need for post-market surveillance.

4. Require notified bodies (i.e., implementors of the regulatory process) to conduct more rigorous surveillance.

As of 2022–2024, all currently approved in-vitro diagnostic devices must be recertified in accordance with the new requirements (TUV Sud, 2020), which is nothing short of a demanding task.

What is the situation on the reimbursement front?

Unlike in pharmaceuticals whereby drugs are reimbursed by various health insurances, in diagnostics, the test results or reports are covered. To generate a report, laboratories require qualified personnel, various laboratory instruments, test kits addressing a variety of diseases, consumables and software solutions tying all parts up in a consistent service. Reimbursement tariffs as such are an aggregate remuneration based on the level of automation, specific diagnostic technology utilized, specimen required for the analysis, test complexity, one or multiple tests needed to generate the results and setting of use, just to name a few (see later chapters more in-depth overview).

This setup has numerous implications:

1. Cost-based reimbursement: Test reports are being considered as a service that require specific inputs, time, and material to perform.

Reimbursement tariffs are generally set based on the costs required to gain the results. Value-based remuneration centered around the complexity of medical decisions supported, added value in the upstream patient pathway, comparator benefits, outcomes achieved, and savings generated is growing but not yet a mainstream approach.

2. Nonbrand specific reimbursement: Manufacturers develop and commercialize various diagnostics instruments (e.g., Abbott™ ARCHITECH™, Roche-Cobas®, Siemens–Atellica®) that run a wide portfolio of tests addressing a variety of disease questions. Troponin, for example, measures the level of cardiac-specific troponin in the blood to help detect heart injury. Siemens offers High Sensitivity Troponin-I assay (Siemens Healthineers, 2020), so does Abbott (Abbott, 2020) and bioMerieux (bioMerieux, 2020). Generally, reimbursement tariffs do not differentiate amongst various brands. In fact, tariffs often operate with a generic description, such as "Immunological detection of troponin I and/or troponin T on a ready-made reagent carrier in the case of acute coronary syndrome (ACS), possibly including quantitative evaluation using apparatus" (KBV, 2020).

3. Manufacturers do not always play a direct role in reimbursement discussions. Since laboratory results are covered (which are performed by laboratories), diagnostics' manufacturers are not always part of reimbursement discussions. They might take a supporting role through medical societies and laboratory interest groups, whose opinions payers might be interested in.

4. Reimbursement pathways are diverse with complex stakeholder groups involved. Diagnostics relevant reimbursement pathways can be centralized (national), regional or local depending on how the healthcare system is structured. Pathways may differ depending on whether a manufacturer or laboratory are interested in public reimbursement or private insurance coverage, whether the test is covered in an inpatient or outpatient setting, whether it is covered under permanent schemes or a temporary pool of funding set aside for innovative products.

    These pathways may entail complex stakeholder structures from various parties, e.g., budget holders, state officials, private insurances, laboratories, physician key opinion leaders, health technology assessment bodies, hospital procurement experts and more. (See later chapters for more in-depth assessment.) Finding the optimal pathway when launching a new diagnostic solution requires thorough investigation, stakeholder mapping and scenario assessment.

5. Inconsistent use of health technology assessments (HTA): Health technology assessment is a multidisciplinary process involving systematic evaluation of safety, efficacy and cost-effectiveness leading to policy or reimbursement decisions (WHO, 2020). Various HTA bodies, e.g., EUNetHTA, IQWiG, and NICE have evaluated complex diagnostic solutions. The number of diagnostics HTAs are increasing, yet they are not as common as in innovative medicines, where prices are higher and it is easier to measure the direct impact of a drug on outcomes versus diagnostics, which might have indirect impact. UK's National Institute for Health and Care Excellence (NICE) has developed a diagnostic specific HTA process, the Diagnostics Assessment Program (DAP), which can be a solid methodological guidance for other agencies. Diagnostics HTA outcomes require more direct link to reimbursement decisions.

6. Cost containment is knocking on the door: Proportionally, in-vitro diagnostics represents a low percentage (<5%) of the total healthcare expenditure. With more complex liquid biopsies, next generation sequencing and comprehensive genomic profiling tests in personalized medicine price tags could go up to $3000 USD per test versus just tens of dollars for a simple HbA1c test. With increasing test prices and more scrutiny in healthcare spending, laboratory diagnostics can no longer escape cost-cutting pressures. In the United States, PAMA (Protecting Access to Medicare Act of 2014) aims to reduce public government reimbursement (Medicare) for IVD tests. The law requires Centers for Medicare & Medicaid Services (CMS) to adjust payment rates every three years based on data that labs collect and report during a six-month period. For the first three years (2018–2020), cuts cannot exceed 10%, and for the subsequent three years (2021–2023), cuts cannot exceed 15% (CMS, 2020).

Chapter Summary

Diagnostic solutions support medical decisions. As more complex and higher risk tests are being developed to assist personalized patient management, both regulatory scrutiny and the need for higher quality clinical evidence are also increasing.

Payers reimburse diagnostic test results or reports that are aggregate costs of multiple elements, such as test kits, laboratory instruments, software solutions, professional staff cost and supporting infrastructure. The reimbursement is usually based on the cost of generating the report and not on the value that it provides in the patient management. Complex reimbursement pathways, less consistent use of HTAs and increasing cost containment measures are challenges to be tackled.

The ultimate question arises: How can novel diagnostics secure rapid, broad reimbursement by demonstrating proven medical value? Before looking at our model, let us review what makes diagnostic solutions special from the market access reimbursement point of view.

Chapter #2 Overview

1. The intended use of a test defines its purpose and has major implications on risk classification, regulatory, clinical data requirements and commercialization. It is important to differentiate between manufacturer-developed "commercial kits" or laboratory-developed tests (LDTs) and/or procedures.

2. The test function and where it plays a role in the patient journey—be it a screening, diagnosis, prognosis, or monitoring tool determines its value proposition.

3. A broad variety of scientific methods can be used to analyze biological samples in large, point of care or novel digital diagnostic devices by laboratory experts, medical professionals or by patients themselves to generate test results.

4. Test results can support decision-making in inpatient, outpatient, specialist, general practitioner and/or in-home settings.

WHAT MAKES DIAGNOSTIC SOLUTIONS SO SPECIAL?

You may think a test is a test and period. Not really. There are quite many nuances that are important to distinguish and make a difference from evidence generation, regulatory, reimbursement and commercial perspectives. In this chapter, I will cover the concept of intended use, type of diagnostic devices, technologies, specimen, setting of use, and shortly, we touch base on the regulatory status. Let's start with the intended use.

Intended use is not a description of product features and specifications but a description of the intended medical use of the test. It is a very important concept, since it will also define the test's risk category, associated regulatory and clinical data requirements, supporting label instructions for use in promotional and sales materials (EU IVDR, 2020).

The intended use usually covers:

- The general description of the device, including its intended purpose and intended users.
- What is to be detected and/or measured.
- Its function, such as screening, diagnosis or aid in diagnosis, prognosis, stratification, monitoring, companion diagnostic, etc.
- The specific disorder, condition, or risk factor of interest that it is intended to detect, define, or differentiate.
- Whether it is automated or not.
- Whether it is qualitative, semi-quantitative or quantitative.
- The type of specimen(s) required.
- The testing population and the intended user.
- In addition, for companion diagnostics, the relevant target population, and the associated medicinal product(s).
- The description of the principle of the assay method or the principles of operation of the instrument.

Let me illustrate the points above with Abbott's Point of Care (i-STAT) Troponin-I example: The i-STAT cardiac troponin I (cTnI) test is an in-vitro diagnostic test for the quantitative measurement of cardiac troponin I (cTnI) in whole blood or plasma. Measurements of cardiac troponin I are used in the diagnosis and treatment of myocardial infarction and as an aid in the risk stratification of patients with acute coronary syndromes with respect to their relative risk of mortality (Abbott, 2020).

Regulatory affairs and the quality assurance of diagnostic solutions is a separate discipline that can easily fill an entire book. An in-depth overview is not in scope for our current book, but from the reimbursement perspective, it is essential to address two main questions:

1. How high is the risk of the diagnostic device? The higher the risk, the more regulatory oversight is required, as such more stringent technical and clinical validation is needed.

2. Who develops and performs the test? Diagnostics manufacturer or a laboratory? Since laboratory results are covered, which are performed by laboratories, diagnostics manufacturers and developers are not always part of reimbursement discussions. They might take a supporting role through medical societies and laboratory interest groups.

When a manufacturer develops a commercial test, they must meet the requirements of the EU's In Vitro Diagnostic Medical Devices Directive (IVDD) and EU regulations In Vitro Diagnostic Regulation (IVDR). In the United States, they must undergo the corresponding approval procedures for IVDs at the Food and Drug Administration (FDA), such as Pre-market Approval (PMA) (Johner Institute, 2019).

On the other hand, laboratory developed tests (LDT) or "in-house tests" (products or procedures that are designed, manufactured, and used within a single laboratory) are subject to different, less stringent oversight, whereby medical laboratories need to fulfill specific quality assurance requirements. In the United States, the Centers for Medicare and Medicaid Services (CMS) are responsible for monitoring the laboratories. In Germany, for example, DAkkS (Deutsche Akkreditierungsstelle)—German National Accreditation Body—or the competent state authorities are in charge. (Johner Institute, 2019)

Recent developments on both sides of the Atlantic challenge why regulatory requirements for a laboratory test should depend on whether it is developed by a laboratory or an IVD manufacturer. Rather they advocate for a transparent risk-based oversight approach, robust quality systems and proof of analytical and clinical validity as the basis for the approval (Johner Institute, 2019).

More stringent and consolidated regulatory frameworks could mean higher evidence requirements, potential boost for health technology assessment concept and reinforcing the important role of the manufacturers in supporting medical societies, laboratory interest groups in coverage and reimbursement discussions.

As a next step, I will explain how certain tests add value to the entire patient management pathway, depending on their position in the diagnostic continuum:

Screening: The main purpose of a screening test is to detect early disease or risk factors for a disease in large numbers of healthy, mostly asymptomatic, but potentially at-risk individuals. Usually, these tests are easy to perform and generally designed for high sensitivity (not to miss a potential disease). From the reimbursement perspective, affordability is a key attribute, since benefits (e.g., early detection and intervention) should justify the costs of screening large numbers of potential cases (Health Knowledge UK, 2020). Prevalence, along with test performance, are key determinants of the utility of the screening test. It is desirable to be able to define the target population of a screening test in such a way that the disease prevalence in the test population is high enough to justify the benefits (Maxim, 2014). For example, the American Cancer Society recommends that males should discuss prostate cancer screening with their healthcare provider if they are age 50 and above, at average risk of prostate cancer and expected to live for 10 more years, age 45 for men at high risk of prostate cancer (first-degree relative diagnosed with prostate cancer at an early age), or age 40 for men at even higher risk (those with more than one first-degree relative who had prostate cancer at an early age). After this discussion, a prostate-specific antigen (PSA) blood test is recommended for screening, and a digital rectal exam (DRE) may also be conducted (cancer.org, 2020).

Given that the impact of screening is often long-term, and the costs and benefits can occur in the future, from the HTA, Payer perspective discounting (calculating the present values of future costs and consequences) could also play an important role. Examples of actual screening tests include the pap smear for cervical cancer, PSA (and/or digital rectal exam) for prostate cancer, cholesterol levels for heart disease, B-natriuretic peptide test for patients undergoing echocardiography (Maxim, 2014).

Diagnosis: The purpose of a diagnostic test is to establish the presence (or absence) of disease as a basis for treatment or decision to apply more confirmatory tests for symptomatic individuals or those who screen positive. More emphasis is placed on accuracy and precision, and tests are geared towards high specificity to accurately "rule out" true negatives and detect those who need further investigation. They might be more invasive and more expensive (Health

Knowledge UK, 2020). Diagnostic tests need to address a clear unmet need, produce actionable results, and need to be easily incorporated into clinical decision-making.

Prognosis: Prognostic tests help to identify and stratify patients into different risk categories regarding specific future outcomes, for example, the likelihood of developing a disease or experiencing a medical event. For practical purposes, those test results are mostly categorized in simple groups that have treatment implications. "Low risk" group could mean no further evaluation or treatment required; "intermediate risk" may indicate that further tests and monitoring are needed, and "high risk" may trigger immediate treatment or prevention measures.

Measuring the precision and accuracy of outcome probabilities is the primary focus of these tests. The value of the test depends on common performance metrics (e.g., sensitivity and specificity), which may be enhanced with observed outcome probabilities, how the new prognostic test reclassifies patients into different risk categories and improves the predictive accuracy, and therefore, the overall patient outcomes (Rector, 2012).

Examples of prognostic tests include CHA2DS2-VASc score, which was developed to improve stroke prevention in atrial fibrillation (AF), whereby high-risk patients are offered oral anticoagulation treatment to prevent strokes (MDCalc, 2020). The measurement of the Elecsys sFlt-1/PlGF ratio identifies pregnant women who are at high risk of developing preeclampsia (a pregnancy complication characterized by high blood pressure and signs of damage to another organ system, most often liver and kidneys) (Mayo Clinic, 2020). Those at high risk require a closer monitoring, whilst doctors can confidently send patients home if they are classified as low risk, hence saving resources (Roche, 2020).

From the reimbursement perspective, the key questions are how reliably the test can identify certain risk groups and whether the stratified intervention is more favorable from the outcome and cost perspectives than a patient management approach.

Monitoring: These tests take periodic measurements that guide the management of a chronic or recurrent condition. Monitoring tests may determine the stage of disease or can aid decisions to initiate, control, change or stop a treatment. Some examples include blood glucose monitoring in diabetes to manage insulin intake or anticoagulation measurement in atrial fibrillation or heart valve disease to keep patients in check for blood-thinning treatments, like warfarin (Doust, 2013). From the reimbursement perspective, testing duration, frequency of testing and test prices can be concerns, due to potential budget impact.

Diagnostics scientific technologies are also relevant to discuss. Here is a quick guide to decoding the mechanics behind some commonly discussed technologies. I will provide a few relevant examples to illustrate the heterogeneity of the various applications, leading to test results.

ELISA (Enzyme-linked Immunosorbent Assay)—detects the target molecule with an enzyme-labelled antibody. By adding a certain solution to the mix, a color change occurs. The speed of the color change depends on the amount of target molecules present in the solution (ScienceDirect, 2020).

Real time PCR—quantitative Polymerase Chain Reaction (PCR) is a molecular biology laboratory technique. This method is used to quantify the amount of DNA in the sample (ScienceDirect, 2020). Digital PCR is a variant of PCR where the reaction is split up in multiple small reactions. Each of those reactions contains only one DNA molecule. During the amplification, each reaction gives a positive (1) or a negative signal (0) for the target sequence, hence the digital output (Gerdes, 2017).

H&E (Haematoxylin and Eosin Staining) — most cells are colorless and transparent; H&E is an artificial coloration of a cell structure to facilitate examination of tissue under the microscope. Staining usually uses a dye to mark the various cells to different color (University of Leads, 2020).

IHC (Immunohistochemistry)—is a microscopy-based technique to visualize certain cell structures or protein within an antibody on a tissue section (Proteinatlas.org, 2020)

In FISH (Fluorescence In Situ Hybridization)—specific regions of the chromosomes are visualized with a fluorescent probe. When a certain cancer-related abnormality needs to be detected, the respective FISH probe can attach to that region and make the region visible under the microscope, and therefore, allow for a diagnosis (Sciencedirect, 2020).

NGS (Next Generation Sequencing)—also known as high-throughput sequencing technology, allows to rapidly sequence DNA or RNA in parallel, at the same time. Whilst manufacturers use different technologies, the resulting output usually is achieved by preparation of the sequencing library, amplification, and sequencing (ScienceDirect, 2020).

FCM (Flow Cytometry)—is a technology where cells in the solutions are detected with a laser and analyzed based on their size, structure, and surface properties. Based on these criteria, it can be determined whether certain cell types are either overrepresented or underrepresented in the patient sample. This information can be used to make a diagnosis (Labtestsonline.org, 2020).

MS (Mass Spectrometry)—is a technology to analyze components based on their molecular weight.

Very small amounts of proteins or chemical components can be detected and quantified with this method (ScienceDirect, 2020).

After reviewing the various intended uses and scientific technologies to generate test results, let us have a brief look at the instruments that automate the testing procedure. These complex machines operate based on different scientific principles (see above), and they may be found in various laboratory segments (e.g., chemistry, hematology, microbiology, immunology, pathology, cytology). More importantly, they address broad customer needs from the throughput, turnaround time, level of automation (specimen handling and processing, reagent preparation, maintenance) and place of use perspectives.

- High- to medium-throughput instruments analyze large quantities of samples, with very high operational efficiency, usually placed in central laboratories. Leading manufacturers developed families of brands (e.g., Abbott-Architect (Abbott, 2020), Roche-Cobas (Roche, 2020), or Siemens-Atellica (Siemens Healthineers, 2020) to serve a variety of laboratory customer needs with a broad range of devices.

- Point-of-Care solutions (POC) are designed to provide rapid, actionable results at the point of decision, in specific hospital wards (e.g., in infectious diseases), at the general practitioner offices or serving patients directly at home. While the high- to medium-throughput devices are operated by professional laboratory personnel, POC instruments are handled by nurses, physicians, or patients themselves.

  Point-of-Care testing is usually more expensive than testing performed in the central laboratories. In the hospital setting, POC testing might require laboratory support for quality assurance (e.g., support in documentation, results charting and training) (Shaw, 2016). Connecting POC instruments with electronic medical record systems and core laboratory information systems is also essential for the documentation of test results or calculation of risk scores. Abbott's i-STAT (Abbott, 2020), Roche's Accu-Chek® Inform II (Roche, 2020) or Becton Dickinson's Veritor™ Plus System (BD, 2020) are examples for near patient testing solutions.

- With digital transformation, an increasing number of novel diagnostic "devices" are entering the market. Smartphone-based solutions, software as a service diagnostic tools, artificial intelligence-powered decision support software, and complex prognostic algorithms represent a new but dynamically growing segments. Policy makers, regulators, and payers already understand the significance of these innovative technologies and aim to enable adoption by engineering favorable policy environments.

Diagnostic devices require biological specimens to perform the laboratory analysis. The sample used for testing is often determined by the purpose of the test. Common examples include throat swabs, sputum, urine, blood, serum, plasma, stool, cerebrospinal fluid, or tissue biopsies. Some samples can be easily obtained as the body naturally eliminates them. Blood specimens are obtained by minimally invasive needle puncture, while collection of tissue specimens is a more complex process and may require a local anesthetic and trained medical professional (AACC, 2020).

The test results can support decision-making in various healthcare settings, such as:

1. Hospital inpatient settings, where the patient requires (longer) hospital stay.
2. Hospital outpatient settings, without overnight stay.
3. At specialist medical practitioners' practices (e.g., cardiologists) or at general practitioners (GP) practices.
4. At home, e.g., patient self-testing for chronic conditions' management (e.g., diabetes).

It is crucial to pay close attention to the setting as financing mechanisms and stakeholders to be engaged differ per setting.

Chapter Summary

In summary, to gain successful reimbursement, the following attributes of a diagnostic test should be considered.

First and foremost, the intended use, risk classification and the nature of the test developer needs to be critically analyzed. The test's function as screening, diagnosis, prognosis, or monitoring tool further defines its value proposition and prompts potential reimbursement challenges and optimal approaches. The underlying scientific technology, laboratory disciplines and instruments are also important traits to keep in mind. Defining the setting of use and the key users will help to identify the optimal reimbursement pathways and key stakeholders, which I will address in the next chapter.

Chapter #3 Overview

1. Reimbursement drives access to diagnostic solutions.

2. Diagnostic solutions can be paid directly by patients via out-of-pocket payments or indirectly via various mandatory or voluntary health insurance options. In many developed countries, private health insurance often supplements public insurance and covers co-payments, deductibles, and specific services.

3. In an inpatient setting, most of the time, hospital laboratories would perform the diagnostic tests. They operate under global budgets and negotiate with suppliers on diagnostic instruments, tests, and consumables.

4. In an outpatient setting, national and/or regional tariff schedules govern test coverage.

5. Reimbursement via tariff schedules offer long-term coverage. To facilitate access to novel (digital) diagnostic solutions, there

Chapter #3 Overview

is a growing number of temporary funds that provide limited, conditional coverage to innovative solutions.

6. Manufacturers, laboratory experts, and physicians can request the coverage, based on their medical and professional needs. HTA bodies evaluate and formulate recommendations from clinical and economic perspectives, while public and private health insurance funds and hospital management decide on diagnostics' coverage, price, or budget. The manufacturer can play a direct role in the submission or may indirectly assist all these stakeholders, with supportive technical, clinical, and economic evidence.

WHAT ARE THE KEY REIMBURSEMENT PATHWAYS & STAKEHOLDERS?

Reimbursement pathways and key stakeholders involved are the most crucial elements in the entire framework. As in every journey: (1) We choose our destination first and define where we would like to be; (2) Draw a map to illustrate how we intend to get there; (3) Then plan and enjoy the trip based on the time, resources, feasibility, and other requirements.

In this first chapter of the framework, I will cover the major diagnostics reimbursement pathway archetypes and key stakeholders involved, mainly organized around four key questions:

1. Who bears the healthcare expense?
2. In what setting is the diagnostic solution utilized?

3. How decentralized is the funding model?

4. How long would the reimbursement or coverage last?

Diagnostic solutions can be paid by either of the following:

1. Patients via out-of-pocket payments.

2. Indirectly via various mandatory or voluntary health insurance options.

State-run health insurances (public system) collect their "revenues" mainly from taxes, while many healthcare systems delegate the day-to-day insurance management to for-profit organizations (private systems), which collect revenues from deductibles and premiums. Those health insurance models and plans can differentiate what medical services are covered and what percentage of claims are borne by the patient (co-payment). The combination of the private and public models is also common.

In industrial nations, healthcare financing has historically been inspired by the following major models:

1. The German "Bismarck model" (professional enrollment through compulsory contributions from employers and employees).

2. UK's Beveridge model (public health monopoly, ensuring universal social protection).

3. A mixed system from United States, where health insurance is not compulsory (OECD, 2020).

In many OECD countries, private health insurance is supplementary to the public scheme and covers co-payments, deductibles, or specific services. The United States and Switzerland have opted for a highly privately financed system. (Switzerland is privately funded, but insurance is compulsory.) While in Germany and in the Netherlands, affluent independent workers and most civil servants can also take care of their own health insurance (OECD, 2020).

Reimbursement schemes can enable access to diagnostic solutions. The wider the patient eligibility and the higher insurance coverage is, the broader diagnostics access can be achieved. The biggest opportunity is usually in the public reimbursement, followed by the private and/or alternative reimbursement schemes, while out of pocket financing is a less favorable option. Depending on which reimbursement pathway we target, there are major implications on the type of stakeholders (government authorities, for-profit businesses) to be addressed, their ways of working (e.g., processes, incentives, timelines), their evidence requirements and preferred ways of communication.

In the previous chapter, we identified four relevant settings where diagnostic solutions can be used. From the reimbursement perspectives, two major avenues should be explored, namely inpatient and outpatient settings (also covering home use).

Inpatient settings—In the inpatient hospital setting, diagnostic tests are usually performed in the hospital's own laboratory. This laboratory operates as an internal organizational unit, cost or profit center, and manages its own operating budget that is allocated through internal budgetary decisions by the finance, laboratory, and medical managers.

Budget planning in the laboratory usually entails costs for human resources, building, instrument operating expenses, test kits and consumables. The management is aware of their operating expenses, future investment needs, requested test types and volumes. They can thus forecast an operating and investment budget.

When a test order arrives, the laboratory performs the request and reports the order in the internal controlling, accounting system for cost allocation purposes. Usually, no specific financial transaction takes place since the laboratory operates under a "global" budget. Should there be an increased demand for certain tests or new innovative tests requested by the treating physicians, laboratory managers can apply for budget adjustments or make investment cases accordingly.

The hospital, in turn, is funded by diagnosis-related group (DRG)-based payment system. The DRG system is a patient classification system (based on various elements: e.g., diagnosis, treatment, length of stay, surgical procedures performed, comorbidities, complications, age, sex). These elements result in complex payment calculations that cover all inpatient charges from the time of admission to discharge (Mihailovic, 2016).

In the hospital setting, diagnostics' manufacturers supply various instruments and tests in multi-year contracts usually awarded through complex tenders. Those tenders can cover: (1) instruments; (2) instruments, tests and consumable bundles; or (3) tests alone. They can be structured as a simple one-off sale, an instrument lease, a rental or a pay-per-test, to name a few options.

In the hospital setting, individual test reimbursement is less relevant. Instead, the emphasis is on the laboratory's global budget and bundled diagnostics' offering. Once the test is approved by the regulators, and there is a physician, patient need to order it, and it is available in the laboratory, reimbursement or funding becomes less of a challenge. Since the hospital manages the entire clinical pathway and bears financial consequences within the DRG setting, it is easier to demonstrate the test's contribution to upstream patient benefits through, e.g., earlier diagnosis or optimized surgical intervention.

Outpatient settings—the outpatient setting has a different reimbursement principle. Usually, tests performed in the outpatient or in-home settings are reimbursed through a tariff catalogue. There is a long list of diagnostics services with associated reimbursement tariffs. These tariffs are documented in specific lists that articulate the test, reimbursement price and indication for each tariff. Examples of tariff lists include Germany's EBM (Einheitlicher Bewertungsmassstab) (KBV, 2020), France's NABM (Nomenclature des Actes de Biologie Médicale) (Ameli, 2020), Switzerland's AL–(Analysenliste) (BAG, 2020) or the Clinical Laboratory Fee Schedule in the United States (CMS, 2020).

These tariffs are maintained by professional bodies who govern the structure of the list, test inclusion, exclusion, patient group eligibility and reimbursement tariffs. Those tariffs can be regularly updated, like in Germany and Switzerland (e.g., yearly, or quarterly), or reviewed on an on-demand basis, like in France. When a test is performed in the GP's office in a point-of-care device or the sample is sent to a bigger laboratory for analysis, the laboratory charges the price based on the tariff schedule.

Those lists mostly govern the public reimbursement segment, but some countries, e.g., Germany, also (partially) regulate the private and out-of-pocket setting, like GOÄ (Gebührenordnung für Ärzte) (PKV, 2020) or IGeL (Individuelle Gesundheitsleistungen) (DKFZ, 2020). On the flip side, the UK does not govern diagnostics' reimbursement tariffs in the public setting, but the CCSD (Clinical Coding & Schedule Development Group) Schedule contains the standard codes for procedures and diagnostic tests for the UK private healthcare sector. This group is managed by private health insurance companies, such as Aviva, AXA Health, Bupa and VitalityHealth (CCSD, 2020).

Outpatient diagnostics reimbursement can be also characterized from the geographical perspective. There are two major models:

1. The national, centralized model.
2. The regional/local, mostly decentralized model.

Germany's EBM and France's NABM are good examples of the centralized model, where one tariff list is applicable for the entire country, while in Spain or Italy, the regional, local healthcare setting is more relevant. In Italy, for example, NTASA nomenclature (Nomenclatore Tariffario dell'Assistenza Specialistica Ambulatoriale) (Ministero della Salute, 2020) provides country tariff guidance, but regional tariffs, such as Veneto's (Regione del Veneto, 2020), are much more applicable on an operational level.

Centralized and decentralized models make a considerable difference in how to approach a reimbursement strategy. In the centralized model, there are a limited number of stakeholders to engage with, usually in a lengthy process with detailed dossier submission and in-depth data requirements. On the flipside though, once the process is successfully completed, the broad coverage could compensate for the efforts invested, but an unfavorable decision can block patient access significantly.

In the decentralized model, there are more local stakeholders to convince, in a shorter amount of time with a less complicated evidence package. The "reward" is also proportional, but a potential negative decision can be also mitigated by approaching other entities.

The duration of the reimbursement coverage is also relevant to assess. The above-mentioned tariff schedules (e.g., Germany—EBM, France—NABM, Switzerland—AL) have been operating for a long time, and once diagnostic solutions are included, they are covered for an extended period and may be removed only when obsolete.

For novel digital diagnostic solutions, however, there are various innovative, alternative funding pathways that offer temporary and limited coverage to facilitate access. These reimbursement options are mostly conditional on additional evidence generation and gaining further clinical experience with the technology. Since there is a variety of innovative pathways, some which can also cover medical devices, I mention a few illustrative examples below:

- In France, RIHN (Le référentiel des actes innovants hors nomenclature de biologie et d'anatomopathologie), for example, sets next generation sequencing tariffs (Ministere des Solidarites et de la Sante, 2020), while the ETAPES program supports the deployment of telemonitoring projects (Ministère des Solidarités et de la Santé, 2020).

- In Germany, the Digital Supply Act (DVG) (Bundesministerium für Gesundheit, 2020) covers certain digital health solutions. Selective contracts may be negotiated between health insurance funds and service providers, providing individual, regional, and time-limited coverage for novel solutions, such as quantitative CRP tests in point-of-care within the context of rational antibiotic therapy (Deutsches Ärzteblatt, 2019).

- In the UK, the cancer and rare disease related genomic tests are centrally funded by

NHS England. The National Genomic Test Directory specifies the tests that are eligible for coverage (NHS England, 2020).

Now that we have a better understanding of what the key diagnostics reimbursement options are, let us take a closer look at the stakeholders who operate, participate in, or influence those reimbursement decisions.

We will review public and private hospital payers, health technology assessment bodies, laboratory, and medical associations. Each of them has an important role in the entire reimbursement process. Laboratory experts and physicians request the coverage, based on their medical and professional needs. HTA bodies evaluate and formulate recommendations from clinical and economic perspectives, while public and private health insurance funds and hospital management decide on diagnostics coverage, price, or budget.

The manufacturer may support all these stakeholders with supportive technical, clinical, and economic evidence. The broader the requested reimbursement is, the more complex the decision-making structure, processes, required technical, clinical and economic evidence are, and the longer the process takes.

Centralized, National Reimbursement Tariffs

Centralized, national reimbursement tariffs: One of the main funding pathways is to be included in a centrally managed, outpatient reimbursement tariff schedule (e.g., EBM, NABM, AL). These tariffs are "owned" and maintained by various government entities, public bodies, or umbrella organizations.

In Germany, for example, the National Association of Statutory Health Insurance Physicians, KBV (Kassenärztlichen Bundesvereinigung), manages EBM (KBV, 2020). In Switzerland, the Federal of Public Health (BAG, 2020) is in charge of the Analysen Liste. In France, the Ministry of Health oversees the NABM, mainly through the National Health Authority (HAS) (Chevreul K, 2010).

Those organizations have assembled professional, multi-disciplinary committees, such as BewA (Bewertungsausschluss) in Germany, CEAP (Commission d'évaluation des actes professionnels) in France, or EAMGK (Eidgenössische Kommission für Analysen, Mittel und Gegenstände) in Switzerland, to make inclusion recommendations.

The list of evaluation criteria can include a broad list of topics, e.g., disease background, epidemiology, technology technical description, implementation in practice, clinical application areas, quality assurance, cost and supporting clinical studies. Based on the novelty of the application, these advisory boards might also request more in-depth health technology assessments and can (or must) align with payer organizations, like National Union of Health Insurance Funds, UNCAM (Union nationale des caisses d'assurance maladie) in France.

Once the committees formulated their recommendations, the decision makers usually endorse them and publish the results in the respective catalogues. The evaluation process is usually complex and can take up to 2–3 years (or longer). Despite the complex list of stakeholders, the key is to look for therapy area experts who can support the case. The payer and medical fraternity operates on evidence and recommendations from trusted colleagues, especially those who are authorities in their area of expertise.

Public and Private Health Insurance Funds

Dealing with public and private health insurance funds is conceptually similar. Based on the medical need, a manufacturer, a laboratory, or physician organizations can make a case for diagnostics coverage within the jurisdiction of the selected insurance company.

Since private health insurance companies are mostly for-profit entities that also compete and aim for customer differentiation, they are slightly easier to approach and faster in decision-making. Nonetheless, they also rigorously evaluate the clinical and economic benefits before making a coverage decision.

Private coverage pathways can be beneficial to secure partial coverage faster by addressing specific needs of an insured population. In certain care settings, selective contracting is a viable solution for securing coverage. In diabetes management, for example, the German AOK Nordwest (Payer) embarked on comprehensive Diabetes Disease Management Program (DMP) in collaboration with Roche Diabetes Care (Manufacturer) and the North Medical Association (Physician)(Aerztezeitung.de, 2019).

Hospitals

Hospitals also operate multidisciplinary teams to procure medical products and services, including laboratory diagnostic solutions. Those teams consist of physicians, nurses and physician assistants, hospital purchasing agents, finance team members, clinical engineers, and laboratory professionals.

Depending on the size of the organization and procurement ticket size, hospital administrators, CEO, CFO, and CMO can also be key stakeholders. Those experts aim to support purchasing decisions with limited budget impact that are cost-effective and provide the best quality outcomes for service users.

Effective procurement follows clear commissioning guidelines and transparent processes. Larger purchases, especially in public hospitals, are procured through tenders. The tender specifications clearly describe the scope of the laboratory products and services to be acquired. The tender process usually follows the following high-level steps:

1. Sourcing vendors.
2. Soliciting bids through Request for Proposals, Quotation, or Invitation to Bid.
3. Bid evaluation along complex criteria system.
4. Contracting (WHO, 2017).

Hospitals and local health authorities can also opt for mini or rapid health-technology assessments to support decisions concerning the introduction of a new health technology. Rapid- or mini-HTAs are quite common in Sweden and Norway (Medtek Norway, 2017).

Since hospitals are major customers of laboratory manufacturers, therefore, direct engagements, sales pitches, product demonstrations with the laboratory professionals, physicians and key decision makers are possible. The bigger the procurement ticket size is, the more complex documentation and evidence package needed.

Laboratory and Medical Associations

Laboratory and medical associations play a pivotal role in securing coverage for diagnostic solutions.

They pull together and organize interests of various clinical laboratory and medical professionals. Since treating physicians and laboratory experts are the ultimate users of diagnostic solutions, it is key to understand their unmet needs to successfully introduce new in-vitro diagnostic tests or instruments. They can also be key advocates for a solution, either to payers or hospital management, once they are convinced of the need for it. Manufacturers can directly engage with them to demonstrate the benefits of their solutions, to generate clinical evidence, to test usage in daily clinical practice or to initiate coverage submissions. In Germany, the 17 regional Associations of Statutory Health Insurance Physicians are a good example.

Health Technology Assessment Bodies

As mentioned in the diagnostics challenges section, health technology assessments are not yet routinely applied in in-vitro diagnostics.

There is a growing amount of analysis in antibiotic stewardship, breast cancer tumor profiling, blood glucose self-monitoring, Vitamin D or NIPT. EU-NetHTA on European level, Federal Office of Public

Health (FOPH) in Switzerland, Institut für Qualität und Wirtschaftlichkeit im Gesundheitswesen (IQWiG) in Germany or NICE's Diagnostics Assessment Program (DAP) carried out those assessments.

Those organizations either foster scientific collaboration and capacity development on EU level or they perform evaluations to support access (e.g., Preeclampsia NICE assessment (NICE, 2016), re-evaluate test inclusion under compulsory health coverage (e.g., Vitamin D in Switzerland (BAG, 2020) or back reimbursement decisions (e.g., Oncotype DX Breast Recurrence Score® in Germany (KBV, 2019). They operate under well-defined processes and methodologies, where manufacturers can be directly or indirectly involved in scoping meetings, through dossier submission or via public consultation. For illustration purposes, UK's NICE Diagnostics Assessment Program (DAP) is worth a further in-depth look (NICE, 2020).

Due to the additional clinical and economic evidence generation, HTAs can be cumbersome for smaller manufacturers. Large organizations, developing complex, differentiated, high-risk diagnostic tests may benefit from them. HTA bodies have an important advisory or "gatekeeper" role in the entire reimbursement process. With the increasing European regulatory scrutiny and evidence requirements, there is a high likelihood that diagnostic HTAs will play an increasing role in securing coverage.

Chapter Summary

Diagnostic tests with a strong medical need are usually covered by some type of public or private health insurance. The majority of the tests are either used in the hospital inpatient setting or in the outpatient setup (including home use).

Laboratory hospitals are generally funded by the broader hospital budget, and diagnostics' manufacturers supply their solutions through tenders or direct negotiations. Tests performed in the outpatient or in-home settings are covered through a tariff catalogue, a long list of diagnostic services with an associated tariff. Those mechanisms are either operated centrally, on a national level or regionally.

Once the diagnostic test is included in the tariff list, it benefits from a long-term coverage. To facilitate early access to innovative diagnostic solutions, there are various innovative, alternative funding pathways that offer temporary and limited reimbursement. Multi-stakeholder expert groups are involved in coverage decisions from the laboratory, clinical, contracting and financing perspectives. The broader the requested reimbursement is, the more complex the decision-making process is.

Extensive clinical and economic evidence is necessary to support their choice. In the next chapter, let me introduce how to demonstrate the medical and economic value.

Chapter #4 Overview

1. Diagnostics' value is relative and very much context specific. It depends on the impacted stakeholders, the patient population in which the test is being applied, alternative solutions that are being compared with, and its indirect impact on the broader care pathway.

2. Diagnostics indirectly influence clinical, emotional, social, cognitive and behavioral patient outcomes. They also impact healthcare resource use and may result in workflow benefits that drive associated costs.

3. The clinical impact of a diagnostic test is characterized by analytical validity, clinical validity, and clinical utility. Clinical and economic evidence generation is usually in alignment with the test's associated patient's risks, its novelty, and healthcare providers' familiarity with the product. The newer and riskier the test, the more clinical and economic evidence is required.

Chapter #4 Overview

4. Economic assessments are often methodologically complex because diagnostics may not directly, but indirectly, impact outcomes in the entire care pathway. As such, biomarkers require comprehensive models to deal with all possible test–intervention combinations in target patient populations.

5. Due to high volume and frequent testing, screening, and monitoring tests may trigger budget impact concerns. Diagnosis and prognosis solutions aim to optimize healthcare resource use by improving treatment or more invasive diagnostic decisions.

HOW TO DEMONSTRATE DIAGNOSTICS MEDICAL & ECONOMIC VALUE

Now that we have reviewed the key diagnostics reimbursement pathways and stakeholders, we shall also cover how to demonstrate the clinical and economic benefits of the diagnostic solution in scope.

In this chapter, we will review the key factors influencing a diagnostics test value, the types of clinical and nonclinical impact that diagnostics can make, followed by the economic value of screening, diagnosis, prognosis, and monitoring solutions. The chapter does not specifically aim to introduce detailed health technology assessment requirements but rather represents a broader context. Nonetheless, in specific sections of the book, some HTA specific examples and implications are highlighted.

Value is always relative. A diagnostic test can represent completely different value drivers for a laboratory expert (e.g., accuracy, workflow improvement, turnaround time), for a physician (e.g., faster, better diagnosis, leading to optimal care selection), for a patient (e.g., faster intervention and recovery, longer and healthier life) or for a public health agency (e.g., optimal population-based screening strategy). Since this book covers the reimbursement, payer perspective, there are two main aspects to highlight, namely clinical and the economic benefits of the diagnostic solution versus standard of care in a specific patient, disease, and care delivery setting.

Take a generic biomarker, like the C-Reactive Protein (CRP), for example. It can signal a serious infection or other disorder. The CRP test can be used in different disease and patient settings, such as sepsis, inflammatory bowel disease, an autoimmune disorder like lupus, rheumatoid arthritis, or a bone infection, e.g., osteomyelitis (MedlinePlus, 2020). The CRP test can be performed in a high-throughput centralized laboratory, in a point-of-care setting (e.g., GP or pharmacy) conducted by a healthcare professional or in an at-home setting by the patient themselves.

To have a complete overview of the key factors influencing diagnostics test value, let me borrow a few points from NICE's Diagnostics Assessment

Program Manual (NICE, 2020) and AdvaMed's Framework for Comprehensive Assessment of the Value of Diagnostic Tests (Advamed, 2017).

Patient population: As we have already discussed in the intended use section, the diagnostic test can support medical decisions in various ways (screening, diagnosis, prognosis, monitoring), leading to interventions that directly affect patient-relevant outcomes. Since patient groups are very heterogeneous and defined by a broad variety of characteristics (e.g., disease probability, causes, stage, severity, comorbidities, age, gender, genetic risk factors), patient selection for value demonstration and capture is pivotal.

Intervention and comparator: Various diagnostic technologies, the intended use, and the setting of use also makes a difference in delivering value. Novel technologies never operate in the "vacuum," but they offer certain benefits in relation to comparators that are most used in existing practice. Understanding current care and choosing the right comparator is essential in estimating the value of a novel technology.

Care pathway: Diagnostic tests provide valuable insights to optimize the care pathway. Take for example, the HbA1c test in diabetes. A value of >7% indicates that a patient is at higher risk of microvascular complications and deserves more medical attention, whereas a value of <7% signals good control of the disease (WebMD, 2021). To define value, one must consider the broader disease context, diagnostic sequences and what these might entail (avoidance of certain treatments, and therefore, costs; early detection of disease, and therefore, avoiding complication costs, etc.).

Implications can include: (1) short- and long-term health benefits and harms (including the true and false results); (2) emotional, social, cognitive, behavioral, and informational outcomes (e.g., the relief of anxiety). The associated costs and healthcare utilization mirror the care pathway, comparators, and health outcomes.

Depending on the technology and intended use, a test may be integrated into the care pathway as replacement, triage or add-on tests (Ludwig Boltzmann Institut, 2014). (1) The replacement test usually maintains the same performance while increasing cost-effectiveness or reducing adverse events; (2) Triage tests aim to avoid invasive or expensive procedures by decreasing unnecessary referrals; (3) Add-on tests refine a diagnosis with the goal to improve treatment decisions, and thus, outcomes.

The clinical impact of a diagnostic test is influenced by multiple factors, namely, analytical validity, clinical validity, and clinical utility.

- Analytical validity ensures that the test not only provides one-off results but also that it is repeatable, reproducible, and able to measure the analyte or biomarker consistently (Leeflang, 2019).
- Clinical validity is the accuracy of the test to identify a particular clinical condition in each patient group. It is described by sensitivity (how often a test accurately generates a positive result for people who have the condition), specificity (how often a test accurately generates a negative result for people who don't have the condition), positive predictive value (probability of having the disease of interest in a subject with positive result), and negative predictive value (probability of not having a disease in a subject with a negative test result) (Leeflang, 2019).
- Clinical utility measures to what extent the test results change diagnostic reasoning and decision-making, leading to improved patient outcomes after testing (Leeflang, 2019).

Generating high-quality evidence is a prerequisite to demonstrating and capturing the value of various diagnostic solutions. Since clinical and economic evidence generation can be an expensive and long undertaking, and the level, quantity, and type of clinical studies should be in alignment with the test's associated patient risks, its novelty, and healthcare providers' familiarity with the technology.

Various types of evidence can be applied in the diagnostics' settings. These include prospective cohort studies with and without comparators using patient registry data, retrospective studies utilizing medical records and claims data, case studies, meta-analysis, and consensus statements (Advamed, 2017). Randomized controlled trials (RCTs) are the gold standard for assessing the effectiveness and safety of various interventions, yet due to high associated resources, required sample size and complex interdisciplinary teamwork are not so often conducted in the evaluation of diagnostic tests. Instead, cohort studies are commonly performed (Rodger, 2012).

From the economic value demonstration perspectives, we shall differentiate between patient and outcome relevant costs and resource use (e.g., unit costs of diagnostics, treatments, surgical methods, hospital readmissions, length of stay) and healthcare system, workflow relevant metrics, such as wait times, frequency of retesting, hours of operations and training needs.

Economic assessments are often methodologically complex because diagnostics indirectly impact outcomes in the entire care pathway, and as such, biomarkers typically require comprehensive models to deal with all possible test/treatment combinations in various populations (Oosterhoff, 2016). Let us review the economic value demonstration characteristics in screening, diagnosis, prognosis, and monitoring:

Screening

The aim of screening is to reduce disease-specific morbidity and mortality through early intervention. Screening programs are efficient when:

1. The target disease is a substantial health problem.
2. The treatment is available, and the program provides better outcomes.
3. The disease can be diagnosed in an early, presymptomatic stage.
4. The precise screening test and adequate infrastructure exist to detect the target disease.
5. The cost of a screening program is in relation to total costs of a disease (Krauth, 2010).

These programs usually measure the number of detected cases with illness, distribution of disease stages (especially in cancer), survival time and mortality in the screened and control group. From reimbursement perspectives, affordability is a key attribute, since benefits (e.g., earlier detection, intervention, and prevention of complications) should justify the costs of screening large number of potential cases. Likely positive health outcomes may occur much later than the time of the screening, therefore, longer time horizon and discounting should be applied (Krauth, 2010).

Diagnosis

Diagnosis can establish the presence (or absence) of disease as a basis for treatment or more invasive diagnostic decisions.

In heart failure (HF), accurate and timely diagnosis is crucial to ensure patients receive appropriate treatment and avoid hospital admissions. Diagnosing heart failure can be difficult as signs and symptoms commonly overlap with other conditions (Taylor, 2010). The natriuretic peptide (BNP) is a useful biomarker to make diagnosis more accurate and efficient by ruling out HF. More accurate diagnosis may lead to reduction in the number of echocardiograms; reduction in patients staying in a hospital to wait for an echocardiogram to confirm/refute their diagnosis; more appropriate/timely referral to a specialist HF team; improved treatment and management and shorter length of hospital stay, to name a few (Heart Failure Hub Scotland, 2015 November). In early rule-out of acute coronary syndrome (ACS), another very potent biomarker, high-sensitivity cardiac troponin can rule out a larger number of patients, shorten the overall stay and reduce the cost of the emergency department expenses in comparison with the traditional troponins (Lippi, 2017).

Prognosis

Prognostic biomarkers can be used for risk stratification of patients to avoid expensive or invasive treatments and to ensure the optimal distribution of resources.

Prognostic biomarkers may also be used in a screening population to identify people at risk to develop a specific health condition. Test results might induce a change in behavior (e.g., a healthier lifestyle to compensate a high-risk prognosis), as such, emotional, social, cognitive outcomes could be also considered (Ludwig Boltzmann Institut, 2014).

Monitoring

Monitoring could mean frequent testing for a longer period to help managing a chronic condition.

When the condition also impacts many patients, like diabetes, it can impose a large burden on societies and on healthcare budgets. Obvious questions arise: How do those test results contribute to better outcomes? What subgroups benefit the most? And in what setting shall the test happen?

Testing solutions in diabetes monitoring and management went through an evolution from a standalone glucose, HbA1c testing conducted by a healthcare provider to comprehensive digital disease management solutions, where patients actively manage their conditions with remote coaching and physician support. After CMS's significant test strip reimbursement cut in the United States (pharmacist.com, 2013), the message was clear: Payer focus is shifting from "only" measuring glucose levels to "also" using the following to achieve better health outcomes:

1. Continuous glucose monitoring solutions, like Abbott's FreeStyle Libre, which uses a tiny sensor under the skin to measure glucose levels day and night.

2. Coaching platforms, like Omada (Omada, 2020), which is a digital lifestyle change program that uses behavioral medicine techniques to help members lose weight and reduce their risk for type 2 diabetes.

3. Mobile apps/web portals, like Insulia® (Insulia, 2020), recommend basal insulin doses based on a physician set treatment plan.

4. Bundled solutions, like mySugr® (mySugr, 2020), that integrates app, connected blood glucose meters, usage-based unlimited test strips, and remote coaching.

The above-mentioned solutions provide an effective way to manage large diabetes populations at a fixed cost/patient reaching desired health outcome goals, and as such, payers reimburse them with an increasing frequency. For example, mySugr got covered by AOK Bavaria in Germany (mySugr, 2018); Insulia, in France, through the ETAPES program (Voluntis, 2018); and Omada Health by Blue Cross Blue Shield of Minnesota (Medcitynews, 2019).

Chapter Summary

Diagnostics' value is relative and very much context specific. A test can provide completely different benefits for a patient, physician, laboratory expert or for a public health official. The test role in the patient management pathway, considering the available alternatives, can contribute to the well-being of various distinct patient groups.

Outcomes can entail clinical, emotional, social, cognitive, behavioral elements that influence healthcare resource use, workflow benefits and associated costs. Analytical, clinical validity and clinical utility serve as core layers for supporting evidence needs, supplemented by often methodologically complex economic assessments. Value demonstration is one aspect of defining the price of the diagnostic test. The next chapter will introduce other useful tools supporting diagnostics' pricing.

Chapter #5 Overview

1. There are four principal methods to estimate the likely price of the diagnostic solutions: health economic assessment, willingness to pay studies, analogue assessment, and reimbursement tariff analysis.

2. When defining the price of a diagnostic solution, the test result (service) should be the primary focus, and healthcare system perspective should be accurately applied (reimbursement tariffs, hospital budgets, out of pocket payments or innovative, alternative funding pathways).

3. Comprehensive economic modeling, incremental cost-effectiveness ratio (ICER) and ICER thresholds are useful tools to assess diagnostic value drivers. Willingness to pay (WTP) studies capture the customer perspective in various hypothetical and real-life purchasing scenarios, while analogue assessment uses benchmarking to collect lessons learned.

Chapter #5 Overview

4. One of the most powerful methods is: reimbursement tariff assessment. It shows
   which solutions are reimbursed, at what
   price, which patients are eligible, what
   technology limitations apply and whether
   coverage applies in central laboratory
   and/or point-of-care settings. Reimbursement codes are not exclusive to brand-
   specific manufacturer; they cover technologies, methodologies, or analytes. In very
   specific cases (unique, complex tests with
   high unmet need and supporting evidence), manufacturer product-specific
   coverage might be possible.

WHAT WILL BE
THE LIKELY PRICE?

After reviewing the reimbursement pathway archetypes and how clinical and economical value is captured, the next layer of the framework is defining the likely price of the diagnostic solution in scope. When "triangulating" the pricing recommendation, there are four main methods at our disposal:

1. Defining the value (price) based on clinical and economic value drivers.

2. Running willingness to pay (WTP) studies.

3. Looking at analogue cases, benchmarks.

4. Most importantly, carefully analyzing reimbursement tariffs.

As we transition from options 1 to 4, the price "triangulation" becomes more concrete, factoring in comprehensive value drivers, customer perceptions, commercial aspects, and actual reimbursement tariffs. Since these steps can be quite long and resource intensive, not all steps are necessary. They should be utilized pragmatically, considering the test's novelty, differentiation, and commercial potential. The newer, more differentiated and riskier the test is, the more complete the toolbox should be.

Before going into details about the options above, it is important to revisit the distinction between a manufacturer-developed "commercial kit" and a laboratory-developed test (LDT). For the sake of simplicity, let us call this second option a service. When a diagnostics manufacturer (e.g., Abbott, Roche, bioMerieux) develops a commercial kit, they sell it to clinical laboratories, and those labs perform the test to yield results. The price negotiated between the manufacturer and laboratories or hospitals is the average selling price (ASP) that is defined based on the various deals. For example:

- Instruments
- Tests and consumable bundles
- Tests-alone sales
- Lease
- Rental
- Pay per result

The laboratory then collects the "revenue" based on e.g., outpatient reimbursement tariffs from health insurance companies, from patients or through the "global budget" from the hospitals.

In the case of LDTs (e.g., Oncotype DX®), the service is the laboratory result itself, and the LDT developer gets paid directly mostly through reimbursement tariffs, patient out-of-pocket payments, or alternative funding available through innovation pathways.

In the case of the manufacturer-developed "commercial kit," price setting is rather a business-to-business transaction, keeping in mind the laboratories' incentives to run the tests. While in the case of LDTs, the developer might be directly involved in HTA assessments and coverage discussions. In both instances though the manufacturers, keep in mind the ultimate value/price of the test result (service) relevant to the healthcare system perspective. Let us examine the four main methods.

Clinical and Economic Value Drivers

In the previous chapter, we have introduced how clinical, emotional, social, cognitive, behavioral patient outcomes, healthcare resource use, and workflow benefits may influence the value of the diagnostic tests.

Value can be quantified through comprehensive economic modeling and with the help of incremental cost-effectiveness ratios (ICER) evaluated compared with their corresponding thresholds, (willingness-to-pay value for the outcome of interest, e.g., £20,000 to £30,000 per quality-adjusted life year/QALY in the UK (Gandjour, 2020)).

The shorter the term and the greater the direct medical cost savings are, the stronger those arguments can be translated into actual price arguments.

Willingness to Pay (WTP) Research

This helps to systematically capture what the customers would pay for a product, if given the opportunity to buy it. These studies can be set up in various ways, in hypothetical settings or real ones. They can measure the answer directly or indirectly.

Customers or patients are usually presented with product descriptions and supporting materials through self-administered questionnaires (web-based), instruments, in-person, or telephone interviews.

WTP studies utilize various methodologies, like discrete choice questions, payment cards, bidding games and open-ended questions (Lin, 2013).

Several factors might influence willingness to pay in diagnostic solutions:

1. More severe conditions and diseases without controllable risk factors, (e.g., colon cancer diagnosis and perinatal screening) are examples associated with higher WTP.

2. More accurate tests are also associated with higher WTP as these are perceived to be more useful for medical decision-making and reduce diagnostic uncertainty.

3. WTP study design and elicitation methods also influence results (Lin, 2013).

A research conducted by analyzing 66 diagnostics WTP studies in developed healthcare markets concluded that most reported median WTP values were below $100, mostly representing infectious and sexually transmitted diseases. Most cancer-related diagnostic tests had a median WTP value between $101 to $500, and a few diagnostic technologies relevant to cancer and to expectant parents had a median WTP values greater than $1000 (Lin, 2013).

Analogue Assessment

Analogue assessment involves benchmarking competitors, collecting facts, and deriving lessons learned from historical precedents that help to crystallize pricing and reimbursement strategy in real market conditions.

These assessments can show how similar the solutions are priced, what clinical and economic evidence they generated, and in which countries did comparators secure reimbursement along what pathways. Moreover, they might also provide insights on what challenges were faced and how they were overcome.

Analogue selection plays an important role. Disease setting, diagnostics technology, likely reimbursement pathways are factors to be considered when choosing the benchmarks. Since not all the above-mentioned information is available in the public domain, desk research could be augmented with expert in-depth interviews.

Reimbursement Tariff Assessment

Out of the four possible methods, from my point of view, this one provides one of the most valuable, practical insights.

It requires some detailed detective work, but it answers if the diagnostic solution is reimbursed, at what tariff, what the limitations are from the applied technology and patient eligibility perspectives, and whether the coverage applies in central laboratory or in point-of-care settings. Keep in mind this method is not perfect either; it is applicable for tests used in the outpatient settings, with existing comparator solutions that are already reimbursed. Let us review a few examples:

In **Switzerland**, for instance the pathology services are covered in TARMED (BAG, 2020), the uniform tariff schedule for outpatient medical services, and comprises of more than 4500 positions. It contains medical and technical services, incurred by the physician him/herself and operating expenses for the practice, infrastructure costs, and staff costs for practice employees.

It is based on a tax point system that corresponds to the costs for both medical and technical services. Tax points are multiplied by the tax point value that the cantons set regularly. The sum of medical and technical services, multiplied by the relevant tax point value, constitute the cost in Swiss Francs that the healthcare provider receives for the relevant services.

Out of the 39 chapters, for example, chapter 37 covers pathology, in which items 37.0410-37.0590 contain histopathology (microscopic examination of tissue to study the manifestations of disease) and 37.0600-37.0710 cytopathology services (examination of individual cells extracted from tissues to determine the cause and nature of a disease) (Tarmed Browser, 2020).

- Cancer-related, tissue-based, next generation sequencing tests, for instance, are covered under the item 37.0570 (Tarmed Browser, 2020) (histopathology/

cytopathology, nonmedical service on hand specialist in pathology: DNA sequencing).

- Since tissue-based diagnostics services require a comprehensive workflow, other positions, such as 37.0210 (histopathology, biopsies, medical services: macroscopic dissection and assessment of tissue samples and surgical specimens, category I), are also added to the workup.

- Primary cervical screening with high-risk human papillomavirus (HPV) is, for example, covered under item 37.0590 (histopathology/cytopathology, nonmedical service: on cell suspension, HPV hybridization using chemiluminescence technology, per case) (Viollier, 2018).

There are ongoing discussions in Switzerland aiming to reform TARMED and introduce a new system, TARDOC (FMH, 2021). In mid-2020, the proposal was submitted to the Federal Office of Public Health for extensive review. Experts predict that TARDOC could be launched in early 2022 (SRF, 2020).

In **Germany**, diagnostic solutions are reimbursed by Statutory Health Insurance (SHI) based on the Uniform Evaluation Scale (EBM), a centralized reimbursement catalogue (KBV, 2020). EBM includes

GP services, specialist medical services and jointly billable services. The following chapters are relevant from our perspective:

- Chapter 11 human genetics.
- Chapter 19 pathology.
- Chapter 32 in-vitro diagnostics in laboratory medicine, microbiology, virology, and infection epidemiology.
- Chapter 32.2 referred as basic diagnostics.
- Chapter 32.3 special laboratory tests, requiring dedicated laboratory medicine expertise to conduct.

To define the right billing category and corresponding tariffs, the diagnostics group, the technology, or analyte (a substance whose chemical constituents are being identified and measured) should be defined by the following questions:

1. Is the test biochemical, immunological, chromatographic, molecular, or microbiological?
2. Does the test utilize ELISA, PCR, Next Generation Sequencing methods? (For a cheat sheet on these methods, see the chapter titled "What Makes Diagnostic Solutions So Special").
3. Does it measure blood gas, lipids, Vitamin D or Troponin I/T? (Rathenberg, 2014).

EBM code 32150, for example, covers "immunological detection of troponin I and/or troponin T on a ready-made reagent carrier in the case of acute coronary syndrome (ACS), possibly including quantitative evaluation using apparatus." This test can be only carried out "if myocardial damage is suspected, if the onset of clinical symptoms was more than 3 hours ago and the decision on how to proceed with the patient cannot be made due to the typical symptoms and a typical ECG result" (KBV, 2020).

In terms of innovation pathways, the Repository of Innovative Acts Outside the Nomenclature of Biology and Pathology (RIHN—Référentiel des actes innovants hors nomenclatures) provides conditional coverage in **France** for innovative diagnostic solutions that are not yet reimbursed under NABM (Nomenclature des Actes de Biologie Médicale), outpatient public reimbursement tariff list. Once a test qualifies for the RIHN, they need to carry out prospective and comparative data collection to validate the clinical and economic utility of the test. After 3 years, the outcome of these trials can facilitate subsequent evaluation by the High Authority of Health (HAS—Haute Autorité de Santé) and potential transition to the NABM for long-term reimbursement.

Eligible tests should be innovative in nature, be in the early launch phase, address high unmet need, represent significant clinical benefit, and reduce healthcare costs. The RIHN is updated yearly in a 6-month cycle, starting in September, and finishing with a publication in March (BO Santé, 2015). The list contains approximately 240 items, structured in 17 sections, like microbiology, immunology, gene amplification and molecular hybridization tests or laboratory diagnosis of hereditary diseases to mention a few (Ministère des solidarités et de la santé, 2020).

Next generation sequencing solutions are, for example, listed in RIHN, and the reimbursement rate depends on the size of the sequencing target < 20 kb (kilo base pairs): €882,90; > 20 kb and < 100 kb: €1.503,9; > 100 kb and < 500 kb: €2.205,9 (Ministère des solidarités et de la santé, 2020).

Diagnostics reimbursement codes are largely not brand specific and not exclusive to specific manufacturer's tests. As shown above, they cover technologies, methodologies, or analytes.

Manufacturer/product-specific coverage can occur in limited cases, where the test or service is so extremely unique, complex, the medical unmet need is high, and the supporting clinical/economic evidence is strong.

After several HTA reviews, Oncotype DX Breast Recurrence Score® that supports the decision for/or against adjuvant systemic chemotherapy in patients with a primary hormone receptor-positive/HER2-

positive and nonmetastatic breast cancer, got covered in Germany at 3,296.50€ under the EBM code 19502. Oncotype DX is the only test that the German Federal Joint Committee (G-BA) included in this context in statutory healthcare, with further ordering limitation, by oncology-gynecologists, specialists in internal medicine, hematology, and oncology (KBV, 2019). The 19502 code does not specifically mention Oncotype Dx but refers to "Biomarker-based test in accordance with No. 30 of Annex I 'Recognized examination or treatment methods' of the Guideline Methods for Contractual Medical Care of the Federal Joint Committee" (KBV, 2019). In 2020, G-BA decided that three additional tests, EndoPredict®, MammaPrint® and Prosigna® will be also covered. The remuneration for the tests is still to be determined (KBV, 2020).

These developments illustrate that exclusivity is still very rare and mostly temporary.

Chapter Summary

Translating value into price can be approached from different angles, starting with health economic assessments, surveying customer's willingness to pay, running benchmark assessments, and most importantly, performing reimbursement tariff analysis.

Tariff analysis is a practical, high-added value option that incorporates several important aspects, such as laboratory discipline, diagnostic technology, biomarker of interest, required specimen, and patient eligibility to triangulate the likely price range for the new diagnostics test in scope. In the next chapter, I will introduce the key steps in securing coverage.

Chapter #6 Overview

1. Securing coverage is a long-term strategic play. Ideally, it starts with an early access assessment, identifying the likely reimbursement setting and key stakeholders involved.

2. Once the key stakeholders are identified, their decision-making criteria and processes should be further explored.

3. The key questions leading to coverage are unmet need, disease burden, medical and laboratory benefits, value for money, budget impact, consequences of not funding and in which patient subgroups does the test have the highest impact.

4. A market access plan is a useful tool to discover hurdles, set reimbursement objectives, milestones and resources required. Alignment with regulatory, clinical, and commercial plans is pivotal.

5. Seeking early scientific advice is valuable to pressure-test key working assumptions and to validate access and clinical development plans.

Chapter #6 Overview

6. When developing the clinical and economic evidence base, conference presentations and publications in scientific journals help to increase the chances of making a successful reimbursement case.

7. It is vital to assess if the manufacturer can directly submit a reimbursement request to the respective payers or can only play an indirect role. If it is the latter, engaging medical or laboratory associations and KOLs is important to secure the buy-in and help advocate for the test post-submission. Lead time should be planned in for engagement efforts. After the submission, developers should explore potential ways to be at least partially involved in the process.

CHAPTER #6

HOW TO SECURE COVERAGE

I n the reimbursement pathways section, we have covered the key stakeholders who are involved in coverage decisions.

Both in public and private outpatient settings, we have identified multidisciplinary laboratory, medical and contracting experts who form various teams or committees to advise decision makers on complex coverage questions. HTA bodies conduct comprehensive assessments and operate with well-defined evaluation frameworks. They plan an important role in backing up more complex reimbursement decisions. Physician and laboratory associations as ultimate users also play an essential advisory role. In the current chapter, we will address how to systematically approach them to support the coverage application and decision process.

Early Access Assessment

Firstly, it is pivotal to understand what the likely setting of use will be (inpatient, outpatient), which then defines the key stakeholders who will be involved in the process (see more about that in the "Reimbursement Pathways and Key Stakeholders" section). This early access assessment is usually based on the diagnostics test intended use or likely scenarios, fit in the patient pathway, PICO (patient, problem or population, intervention, comparison, control or comparator, outcomes) analysis, setting of use and target customers.

Once the likely reimbursement pathways, scenarios and stakeholders are identified, we can work backwards to evaluate what requirements, guidelines, decision-making process, and timelines are involved and how the various parties collaborate.

Depending on whether a medical, laboratory or payer expert evaluates the case, different functional data and evidence are required. The key questions usually include:

- Unmet need: Why do patients need the diagnostic solution, and what problem(s) does the test intend to solve?

- Disease burden: How big is this problem from the humanistic, medical, and economic perspectives?
- Medical and laboratory benefits: How is the new diagnostic solution better than the alternatives in the setting of scope?
- Value for money: How much does the new diagnostic technology cost, and why is it worth it in relation to the comparators?
- Budget impact: Can payers afford to fund it, and what is the potential budget exposure?
- What are the potential consequences of not funding it via the target reimbursement method? Are there alternatives?
- Sub-group analysis: In case budgetary concerns arise, in what patient groups does the diagnostics test perform the best and add the most value?

Those questions seem to be easy to answer on the surface, but in real life, rigorous, scientific argumentation is required to back up the answers. Scientific literature reviews, advisory boards, various clinical trials (see chapter on "How to Demonstrate Diagnostics Medical & Economic Value") or economic assessments are necessary to produce a complete "evidence package." It is essential to do your homework and plan for lead time to assemble answers to all aspects of the application.

In Germany, for example, when the diagnostics technology and mode of action is established, the application for an EBM code is submitted to BewA (Institute des Bewertungsausschlusses) Evaluation Committee (Institut des Bewertungsausschusses, 2020).

The application should contain: (1) administrative information; (2) medical background; (3) disease prevalence and incidence; (4) name of the new laboratory service; (5) current illustration of the analyte; (6) implementation of the new laboratory service; (7) clinical issues/ application areas; (8) analytical framework; (9) comparison procedure; (10) guidelines; (11) quality assurance; (12) cost of the new laboratory service/cost-effectiveness; (13) information on the pivotal studies; (14) bibliography (Institut des Bewertungsausschusses, 2019).

In Switzerland, the TARMED (uniform tariff schedule for outpatient medical services) is evaluated by ELGK (Eidgenössischen Kommission für Leistungen und Grundsatzfragen), the Federal Commission for Medical Benefits and Principles, an 18-expert advisory commission of the Federal Office of Public Health (BAG, 2020).

In the application process, ELGK requests: (1) Description of the new service, current comparators; (2) Regulatory status; (3) Financing in neighboring countries; (4) Epidemiology, current patient management pathway; (5) Indication of use, fit in the patient pathway; (6) Current and estimated volume of use; (7) Service provider and quality assurance; (8) Safety and efficacy supported with relevant clinical evidence; (9) Comprehensive assessment of cost effectiveness, budget impact and savings potential considering the comparators (BAG, 2018).

Hospitals tend to use the Most Economically Advantageous Tender (MEAT) criteria to award tenders. Besides the price, MEAT also includes quality, functionality and other aspects of products and services as part of the evaluation metrics. Boston Consulting Group (BCG) and MedTech Europe (the European trade association) jointly developed the Value Based Procurement (VBP) framework that helps authorities, healthcare organizations and industry to make smarter procurement decisions. The VBP concept takes MEAT to another level by assessing improvement in patient outcomes, reduction in the total cost of care, and benefits for other stakeholders. The concept aims to apply the fundamental principles of value-based healthcare to the purchasing decision of medical technologies, including diagnostics (BCG, 2020).

Market Access Plan

To answer those questions in a coordinated fashion, collaboration amongst regulatory, clinical, market access and commercial functions is necessary. Each function aims to prepare for a successful launch by developing the new test, securing regulatory clearance, conducting the necessary clinical trials, and obtaining reimbursement.

A market access plan is a useful tool to: (a) identify, prioritize key launch access gaps; (b) assess key stakeholders involved; (c) develop HTA, coverage, reimbursement objectives, roadmap, deliverables, anticipated risks: and (d) estimate detailed resource requirements. A comprehensive market access plan that is well synchronized with the regulatory, medical, and commercial strategies can ensure successful, project execution.

Early Scientific Advice

Manufacturers who think strategically and plan reimbursement well ahead of the actual product launch may also seek early scientific advice to support their evidence generation plans, validate certain hypothesis in the functional plans and eventually prepare for future HTAs.

NICE, for example, offers early scientific advice, which enables developers to present a clinical development plan, ask questions on population, trial design, relevant outcomes, comparators, health-related quality of life, data collection, economic analysis, cost -effectiveness modeling, extrapolation, resource use and costs. NICE's experts provide advice to support decision-making and help develop an evidence base, which can be used in future evaluations or discussions with payers/commissioners (Diagnostics North East, 2018).

In 2016, the FDA (Food and Drug Administration) launched the voluntary Private Payor Program. Through this initiative, manufacturers can receive joint feedback from the regulator, private payers, and health technology assessors to develop a more efficient evidence generation plan. Members include Blue Cross Blue Shield Association, Duke Evidence Synthesis Group, ECRI Institute, Humana®, and Kaiser Permanente®, to mention a few (Medcitynews, 2018).

Another method is convening payer or scientific advisory boards. With such boards, manufacturers gather relevant payers/ex-payers and therapeutic experts for early advice on evidence requirements, possible challenges and solutions going forward. Convening a payer or scientific advisory board shall not be a one-time exercise, but they can be utilized in multiple occasions to further validate the key hypotheses during the development process.

Another way to keep iterating on the clinical, access and commercial strategy is to engage in various pilot projects, experiments, with potentially lower stakes. From the reimbursement perspective, a deal with a private payer, with one hospital laboratory, or getting covered by an innovative funding scheme is a great achievement and helps manufacturers and healthcare providers to gain further practical experience with the novel diagnostic test in a real-life setting. Such pilots can also yield real-world evidence and add to the case for national reimbursement.

Generating Clinical and Economic Evidence

Generating the required clinical and economic evidence is the longest and most resource-intensive undertaking in the entire process.

It is beyond the scope of this book to cover this topic in-depth, but the key elements were already introduced in the "How to Demonstrate Diagnostics Medical & Economic Value" chapter. Once the various clinical experiments are conducted and health economic calculations are in place, then presentations on scientific symposiums, conferences and publications in scientific journals increase the chances of acceptance in the reimbursement submissions. High internal validity (how well a study is conducted) and external validity (how applicable the findings are to the real world) are also pivotal, not to mention keeping in mind the perspective of the decision makers. A hospital team might be more interested in exploring the operational aspects and local implications of introducing the test versus a national advisory body deciding a nationwide coverage.

Submission

Once the evidence package is in good shape and the key questions can be answered, the final step is the submission. It is key to know who can officially submit the dossier.

In Switzerland, manufacturers can submit their requests directly to the ELGK, while in Germany associations, professional societies (e.g., physician/manufacturer/professional associations, medical societies) can do so.

In case of hospital tenders and when negotiating with private payers, manufacturers can again play a direct role. With smaller, local entities and technologies with lower budget impact, the submission can be leaner and less rigid as structures are less likely to be well-defined versus a full scale HTA submission. Once the process is running and there are potential ways to be part of it as an active or a passive member, it is important to stay on the case and potentially answer any open questions, provide missing information, or simply mitigate objections.

Chapter Summary

Securing coverage is a resource-intensive, strategic play that requires well-coordinated efforts from regulatory, clinical, access and commercial functions.

Early market access assessment helps to identify the likely reimbursement pathways, key stakeholders involved and required data and evidence needs. A market access plan can help to uncover relevant hurdles to coverage, and most importantly, lay out a roadmap how to overcome them in a timely manner.

Payer or scientific advisory boards may externally validate key assumptions and provide valuable inputs for future adjustments that lead to optimal evidence generation. They all lead up to the ultimate step—producing a convincing submission to payers. The document submitted should cover key questions, such as unmet need, disease burden, medical benefits, value for money, budget impact and any other data specified in the application form, if indeed there is an official one.

As the last step of the framework, we will cover all the tips and tricks that can make or break reimbursement projects.

Chapter #7 Overview

To be successful in the job, I find these 7 tips very useful:

1. Scope the problem diligently.
2. Define the intended use scenarios wisely.
3. Work iteratively.
4. Be a bridge.
5. No evidence, no coverage.
6. Be resourceful and experiment.
7. Stay on the ball.

HOW TO BE SUCCESSFUL AT THE JOB

B y now (hopefully), you have an overview on why diagnostics reimbursement and access matters; what makes diagnostics so special; what the key reimbursement pathways are and who the relevant stakeholders are; how to demonstrate value, triangulate the likely price and secure coverage.

As a last step, let me share a few tips on what will make you successful at the job. This section is a collection of some advice that I wish I had known before starting my previous roles. Some of them are project-relevant and others a list of useful personality traits. These tips are more applicable to diagnostics coverage projects and reflect many years of industry and consulting learnings.

Scope the Problem Diligently

Before developing a proposal for our clients, we spend the largest chunk of effort on scoping the problem, the access, and the reimbursement challenge we should aim to solve. As we have illustrated in the "What Makes Diagnostic Solutions So Special?" and "How to Demonstrate Diagnostics Medical & Economic Value" chapters, diagnostic solutions can be very context-specific, and many nuances need to be considered.

When you are responsible for developing, launching, and commercializing a diagnostic solution, this is your universe; you are working under tight deadlines and need to coordinate with several colleagues and/or your investors who may give you a hard time. You have the urge to run and deliver, fast.

Before you start working on any access project, stop for a second and define the challenge first. What are the problems you aim to solve? What does project success look like? What strategic decisions will you need to support? What geographic area are you interested in? What is the diagnostics technology scope? What level of insights and confirmation is required? These are just a few questions you might like to articulate answers to.

Define the Intended Use
and Likely Scenarios

In early development project phases, there may be several options on how the test could support clinical decisions, how it could fit in the patient pathway, whether the test is quantitative or qualitative. Take your time to define the likely intended use scenarios.

This is the starting point for every reimbursement project. For a comprehensive list of questions that define the intended use, please refer to the "What Makes Diagnostic Solutions So Special?" chapter.

Work Iteratively and Start
With an Early Access Assessment

Product development and commercialization may not always be straightforward; they are rather iterative processes. During the development process, many hypotheses are either confirmed or refuted, and development programs and functional strategies are adjusted as a result.

Bear in mind that scenarios usually get fine-tuned along the way. Early access assessment is a powerful tool to start with. (For more details, refer to the "How to Secure Coverage" chapter.) But do not forget that it is not the plan itself but the planning that matters. Plans are outdated once they are ready, but developing them helps to clarify roadblocks, risks, priorities, and consider options on how to overcome them.

Be a Bridge

Securing reimbursement is an integral part of a well-coordinated product development effort. Working closely with regulatory, clinical, and commercial counterparts is critical.

The intended use, clinical evidence, likely reimbursement price and commercialization efforts are all interlinked. By nature, market access connects various functions. Economic value depends on clinical benefits and intended use, and those also impact the reimbursement price, which has enormous implications on the test's launch and commercialization success. To be successful at reimbursement, you need a curious mind and the ability to articulate things clearly, first to yourself, then to your stakeholders. Exploring and understanding the clinical and commercial aspects helps to excel in the role.

No Evidence, No Coverage

The entire life science industry is about generating clinical and economic evidence to prove that the claimed product benefits work in real life.

Payers require substantial evidence to be confident that they are making the right decisions for the patients and for prudent budgetary purposes. To maximize changes for coverage, work hand-in-hand with the clinical colleagues to design high quality clinical programs with payer-relevant endpoints.

Be Resourceful and Experiment

In comparison to innovative pharmaceuticals, the commercial opportunity for a diagnostic test is significantly smaller. "Commercial kit" manufacturers also aim to optimize the revenue stream from the installed instrument base and not necessarily from one specific diagnostic test perspective.

Lower peak sales and aiming for maximizing the capacity of the installed instruments provide less incentives to select one specific test and to invest significant resources in large scale clinical trials, launch preparation and awareness campaigns. When working on reimbursement projects, a bottom-up, stepwise, "experimentational" approach combined with resourcefulness comes in handy.

Try to first secure coverage in one specific hospital, and aim for a smaller tender submission. Gain coverage in an innovation funding pathway, and negotiate with a private payer before you go all in. This bottom-up approach may help to confirm a few hypotheses, test, and further develop the evidence package.

The goal is to increase adoption in an incremental fashion and make the test more familiar to patients, laboratory experts and physicians in real-world settings.

Stay on the Ball

Reimbursement and market access are still relatively new disciplines in the diagnostics world but with growing relevance. In the last 15–20 years, innovative pharmaceuticals and medical device manufacturers have already incorporated the payer mindset in their product development and commercialization processes.

With the ever-growing importance of diagnostic solutions' medical decision-making, the IVD industry has just recently embarked on this journey, and there are still many challenges ahead. (See the "Why Does Diagnostics Access & Reimbursement Matter?" chapter.) Overcoming these hurdles takes time. Be patient. Success does not come easy and fast, but once it is there, it is even more rewarding.

Chapter Summary

No matter how strong the strategic reimbursement plan is, it may be held back by team members if they do not approach it with the right attitude. When it comes down to it, you will make all the difference when implementing the plan.

To be efficient in your job, follow the 7 tips I just shared.

CHAPTER 8

FINAL THOUGHTS

While I was writing this book, COVID-19 dominated our lives. The year 2020 highlighted how important diagnostics are in managing this devastating pandemic, advising public health measures, or just simply enabling international travel.

Molecular, rapid and antibody tests became almost part of our daily routine to rule out SARS-CoV-2 when having flu-like symptoms, to avoid or shorten quarantines or to measure antibodies for vaccine-induced protection. Diagnostic tests have a pivotal function in determining which medical interventions are optimal for whom.

Though actual therapeutic benefit is directly attributed to medicines and to surgical interventions, these solutions can only work if they are applied to the right patient at the right time. Shall we separately attribute the value to the diagnostic solution or to the medicine? It is not an either/or question. The solution probably lies in the diagnostics-treatment-services comprehensive package that jointly helps to make smarter decisions and to achieve better outcomes at manageable costs.

I am personally a big believer of holistic diabetes patient management solutions that integrate smartphone applications, connected blood glucose meters, remote physician advice, peer coaching and dietary recommendations in a pay-per-outcome model on a monthly or yearly subscription basis. With such digitally enhanced service-based offerings where patients are actively engaged on the platform, outcomes can also be measured in a real-world setting.

Reimbursement decisions require clinical and economic proof. Generating high-quality, real-world evidence is expensive, takes a long time, and diagnostics tests need to be in active clinical practice. Innovation funding pathways that offer temporary coverage conditional to further evidence being generated could facilitate access and help to mitigate those challenges. Further commercial incentives could be awarded to first-in-class manufacturers for absorbing the additional development costs and risks.

Value-based diagnostic reimbursement remains a major challenge to tackle. As we discussed in the "How to Demonstrate Diagnostics Medical & Economic Value" chapter, diagnostic solutions' value contribution is very much context-specific and can have positive impacts in entire care pathway. Today's healthcare systems remain mostly fragmented. Preventive measures, general practitioner, outpatient specialist care, hospital treatments, and after-hospital care are managed as stand-alone silos with their own funding mechanisms. The solution probably lies in a vertically integrated payer-provider organization (e.g., HMO—health maintenance organization) that offers a full suite of medical services to a given insured population under one roof.

With one integrated entity, the incentives are clearly aligned, and the silo mentality is dismantled. State-of-the-art health data capture integration, and analytics are important prerequisites to help quantify the downstream impact of a newly introduced diagnostic solution in the entire care pathway. Estonia's integrated e-Health records, e-Ambulance, e-Prescription, and electronic ID-card ecosystem could be a model to further explore (e-Estonia, 2021).

The diagnostics industry is going through a transformation. There is more regulatory scrutiny, increased evidence requirements and the need for richer, more precise insights to support medical interventions. As personalized healthcare becomes more mainstream and tech companies enter the field, integrated health data and insights will be more readily available. Diagnostics is transitioning from measuring one biomarker in the blood to developing complex personalized algorithms from multiple biological samples, wearable data, and electronic medical records. Reimbursement mechanisms also need to keep up with this development and provide clear predictable pathways and necessary incentives to facilitate broader and faster diagnostics patient access.

CHAPTER 9

NEXT STEPS

If you have arrived on this page after reading this entire book—thank you and congratulations. I hope I have been able to share a simple framework, guiding principles and key important aspects of navigating the reimbursement hurdles for in-vitro diagnostic solutions.

Should you require further support on the topic or you have any diagnostics reimbursement, access, and policy questions, it would be an honor for me and my entire team to help you.

If you already have a specific access challenge in mind, please share it with us here:

Centivis.com/request-proposal

It should take no more than five minutes to complete, and we will keep all your information completely confidential. After reviewing your answers, we will contact you to schedule a complimentary phone call to further clarify your needs and answer all your questions. If you think we are the right partner, we are happy to prepare you a nonbinding, in-depth, tailor-made proposal.

You may also directly schedule a 30–60-minute complimentary call at:

Centivis.com/schedule-a-call

or email:

info@centivis.com

Thank you for your time, and we look forward to connecting with you.

ACKNOWLEDGEMENTS

This book is based on several years of learning from the life science industry and from advising our clients. I could not have written this book alone, therefore, I wanted to say special thanks to a specific group of people who helped me along the way:

Credit goes to my team, to Kah-Shin Cheong-Baden, who helped with the editing and proofreading, and to Anastasios Gkiokas and Hansjoerg Schuetzinger, who supported with fact-checking and reviewing the manuscript. You guys rock; thank you for choosing Centivis.

Special thanks to Mike Capuzzi, from Bite Sized Books, who showed that writing and publishing a shook™ (short, helpful book) is not as scary as it looks at the first sight.

I feel privileged to learn from great mentors and leaders, namely from Laszlo Molnar, Jozsef Bodrogi, Andras Incze, Jens Grueger, Jasper Huels, Jean-Claude Gottraux and Frank Desiere.

This short book would not have been possible without our superb clients and my previous colleagues who helped to establish the framework, connect the dots, and refine the concept along the way.

I owe an enormous debt of gratitude to my mom, dad, uncle, and grandma who gave me all the tools of independence, supported a nurturing childhood, and invested in my education.

Finally, my deepest thanks go to my wife, Nicole, and to my daughter, Julia, for their love, understanding and unconditional support.

REFERENCES

AACC. (2020, November 19). American Association for Clinical Chemistry (AACC). Retrieved from A New Era for Liquid Biopsy: https://www.aacc.org/cln/articles/2020/november/a-new-era-for-liquid-biopsy

AACC. (2020, November 24). Labtestsonline. Retrieved from Collecting samples for laboratory testing: https://labtestsonline.org/articles/collecting-samples-laboratory-testing

Abbott. (2020, November 19). Abbott. Retrieved from High Sensitive Troponin-I: https://www.corelaboratory.abbott/int/en/offerings/assays/troponin

Abbott. (2020, November 24). Abbott. Retrieved from Architect: https://www.corelaboratory.abbott/int/en/offerings/brands/architect

Abbott. (2020, November 24). Abbott. Retrieved from i-STAT: https://www.pointofcare.abbott/int/en/offerings/istat

Abbott. (2020, November 20). Abbott Point of Care. Retrieved from Cardiac Troponin I (cTnI): Cardiac Troponin I (cTnI)

Advamed. (2017). A Framework for Comprehensive Assessment of the Value of Diagnostic Tests. Washington, D.C: Advamed.

aerztezeitung.de. (2019, December 12). aerztezeitung.de. Retrieved from Mehr Selbstmanagement für Diabetiker: https://www.aerztezeitung.de/Nachrichten/Mehr-Selbstmanagement-fuer-Diabetiker-404970.html

Ameli. (2020, November 26). NABM. Retrieved from NABM: https://www.ameli.fr/medecin/exercice-liberal/remuneration/nomenclatures-codage/codage-actes-biologiques-nabm

BAG. (2018, May 22). BAG. Retrieved from Formular Antrag auf Kostenübernahme durch die obligatorische Krankenpflegeversicherung betreffend Leistungen (DOC, 40 kB, 22.05.2018): https://www.bag.admin.ch/dam/bag/de/dokumente/kuv-leistungen/bezeichnung-der-leistungen/Antragsprozesse%20Allgemeine%20Leistungen/antragsformular-betreffend-Leistungen.docx.download.docx/Formular%20Antrag%20auf%20Kosten%C3%BCbernahme%20durch%20die%20oblig

BAG. (2020, November 26). Analysenliste. Retrieved from Analysenliste: https://www.bag.admin.ch/bag/de/home/versicherungen/krankenversicherung/krankenversicherung-leistungen-tarife/Analysenliste.html

BAG. (2020, December 16). BAG. Retrieved from Antragsprozesse Allgemeine Leistungen: https://www.bag.admin.ch/bag/de/home/versicherungen/krankenversicherung/krankenversicherung-bezeichnung-der-leistungen/antragsprozesse/Antragsprozesse-Allgemeine-Leistungen.html

BAG. (2020, November 27). HTA Scoping reports. Retrieved from HTA Scoping reports: https://www.bag.admin.ch/bag/en/home/versicherungen/krankenversicherung/krankenversicherung-bezeichnung-der-leistungen/re-evaluation-hta/scoping-berichte.html

BAG. (2020, December 08). Tarmed. Retrieved from Tarmed: https://www.bag.admin.ch/bag/de/home/versicherungen/krankenversicherung/krankenversicherung-leistungen-tarife/Aerztliche-Leistungen-in-der-Krankenversicherung/Tarifsystem-Tarmed.html

BCG. (2020, January 9). BCG. Retrieved from How Procurement Unlocks Value-Based Health Care: https://www.bcg.com/en-ch/publications/2020/procurement-unlocks-value-based-health-care

BD. (2020, November 24). BD. Retrieved from Veritor Plus: https://www.bd.com/en-us/offerings/capabilities/microbiology-solutions/point-of-care-testing/veritor-plus-system bioMerieux. (2020, November 19). bioMerieux. Retrieved from Vidas High Sensitive Troponin-I: https://www.biomerieux-diagnostics.com/vidasr-high-sensitive-troponin-i

BO Santé. (2015, September 15). BO Santé – Protection sociale. Retrieved from Solidarité no 2015/8: https://solidarites-sante.gouv.fr/fichiers/bo/2015/15-08/ste_20150008_0000_0113.pdf

Breast Cancer Now. (2020, November 19). Breast Cancer Now - The Research and Care Charity. Retrieved from Oncotype Dx: https://breastcancernow.org/information-support/facing-breast-cancer/diagnosed-breast-cancer/oncotype-dx#:~:text=Oncotype%20DX%20is%20a%20test,(see%20Oncotype%20DX%20score).

Bundesministerium für Gesundheit. (2020, November 27). Digitale-Versorgung-Gesetz. Retrieved from Digitale-Versorgung-Gesetz: https://www.bundesgesundheitsministerium.de/digitale-versorgung-gesetz.html

cancer.org. (2020, November 17). cancer.org. Retrieved from American Cancer Society Recommendations for Prostate Cancer Early Detection: https://www.cancer.org/cancer/prostate-cancer/detection-diagnosis-staging/acs-recommendations.html

CCSD. (2020, November 26). CCSD. Retrieved from CCSD: https://www.ccsd.org.uk/

CDC. (2020, November 19). Centers for Disease Controls and Prevention. Retrieved from Divison of Laboratory Systems: https://www.cdc.gov/csels/dls/ strengthening-clinical-labs.html

CENTIVIS. (2019, August 5). Centivis. Retrieved from U.S. Lab Test Reimbursement Rates: What's New(S)?: https://www.centivis.com/news/2019/8/5/us-lab-test -reimbursement-rates-whats-news

Chevreul K, D.-Z. I.-Q. (2010). France: Health system review. Health Systems in Transition. Geneva: WHO. Retrieved from France Health System Review.

CMS. (2020, November 26). CMS. Retrieved from Clinical Laboratory Fee Schedudle: https://www.cms.gov/ Medicare/Medicare-Fee-for-Service-Payment/ ClinicalLabFeeSched

CMS. (2020, December 23). cms.gov. Retrieved from cms.gov: https://www.cms.gov/Medicare/Medicare- Fee-for-Service-Payment/ClinicalLabFeeSched/PAMA -Regulations

Deutsches Ärzteblatt. (2019). Modellprojekt mit CRP- Schnelltest soll gezielte Verordnung von Antibiotika fördern. Deutsches Ärzteblatt, https:// www.aerzteblatt.de/nachrichten/106562/ Modellprojekt-mit-CRP-Schnelltest-soll-gezielte- Verordnung-von-Antibiotika-foerdern.

Diagnostics North East. (2018, April 01). Diagnostics North East. Retrieved from NICE Diagnostics Assess- ment Programme: https:// diagnosticsnortheast.org.uk/wp-content/ uploads/2018/04/Rebecca-Albrow-Web.pdf

DKFZ. (2020, November 26). DKFZ. Retrieved from DKFZ: https://www.krebsinformationsdienst.de/untersuchung/igel.php

Doust, J. (2013). Monitoring in Clinical Biochemistry. Clin Biochem, Vol 34.

e-Estonia. (2021, January 5). e-Estonia. Retrieved from e-Estonia: https://e-estonia.com/solutions/healthcare/e-health-record/

EU IVDR. (2020, November 20). EU IVDR. Retrieved from EU IVDR: https://euivdr.com/

FMH. (2021, January 8). FMH. Retrieved from FMH: https://www.fmh.ch/themen/ambulante-tarife/tardoc.cfm

Gandjour, A. (2020). Willingness to pay for new medicines: a step towards narrowing the gap between NICE and IQWiG. BMC Health Services Research, 20:343.

Gerdes, L. (2017). Digitale PCR. Journal of Consumer Protection and Food Safety, 53–56.

Health Knowledge UK. (2020, November 20). Health Knowledge UK. Retrieved from Differences between screening and diagnostic tests and case finding: https://www.healthknowledge.org.uk/public-health-textbook/disease-causation-diagnostic/2c-diagnosis-screening/screening-diagnostic-case-finding

Heart Failure Hub Scotland. (2015 November). Scottish Heart Failure Hub Business case for the funding of NT-proBNP for the diagnosis and management of patients with Heart Failure in NHS Scotland. Scotland: Drs Clare Murphy.

Institut des Bewertungsausschusses. (2019, July 1). Institut des Bewertungsausschusses. Retrieved from Methodological requirements for the implementation of the standardized assessment procedure according to § 87 Paragraph 3e Clause 1 No. 1 SGB V: https://institut-ba.de/ba/Verfahrensordnung_Kapitel_I_Anlage_3.pdf

Institut des Bewertungsausschusses. (2020, December 15). Institut des Bewertungsausschusses. Retrieved from Institut des Bewertungsausschusses: https://institut-ba.de/institut.html

Insulia. (2020, December 4). Insulia. Retrieved from Insulia: https://insulia.com/

Johner Institute. (2019, January 19). Johner Institute. Retrieved from Laboratory Developed Tests LDT: https://www.johner-institute.com/articles/regulatory-affairs/and-more/laboratory-developed-tests/

KBV. (2019, June 20). KBV. Retrieved from RICHTLINIE METHODEN VERTRAGSÄRZTLICHE VERSORGUNG: https://www.kbv.de/html/42212.php

KBV. (2019, December 19). PRAXISNACHRICHTEN. Retrieved from Kassen übernehmen Kosten für biomarkerbasierten Test bei Brustkrebs: https://www.kbv.de/html/1150_43614.php

KBV. (2020, November 26). EBM. Retrieved from EBM: https://www.kbv.de/html/online-ebm.php

KBV. (2020, November 19). Kassenärztliche Bundesvereinigung. Retrieved from Einheitlicher bewertungsmassstab (EBM): https://www.kbv.de/tools/ebm/html/32150_2902756010390946504000.html

KBV. (2020, November 28). KBV. Retrieved from KBV: https://www.kbv.de/html/426.php

KBV. (2020, December 19). KBV. Retrieved from EBM: https://www.kbv.de/tools/ebm/html/32150_2902756010390946504000.html

KBV. (2020, October 22). PRAXISNACHRICHTEN. Retrieved from Weitere Biomarker-Tests bei Brustkrebs werden Kassenleistung: https://www.kbv.de/html/1150_48821.php

Krauth, C. (2010). Health economic analysis of screening. GMS Curr Top Otorhinolaryngol Head Neck Surg, 1-14.

Labtestsonline. (2020, November 23). Labtestsonline. Retrieved from Flow cytometry: https://labtestsonline.org/flow-cytometry

Leeflang, M. (2019). How to: evaluate a diagnostic test. Clinical Microbiology and Infection, 54-59.

Lin, P.-J. (2013). Willingness to Pay for Diagnostic Technologies: A Review of the Contingent Valuation Literature. Value in Health, 797-805.

Lippi, G. (2017). Clinical, organizational and economic analysis of high-sensitivity cardiac troponin testing in the emergency department. Annals of Research Hospitals,, 1:44.

Ludwig Boltzmann Institut. (2014). Procedural guidance for the systematic evaluation of biomarker tests. Vienna: Ludwig Boltzmann Institut.

Maxim, L. D. (2014). Screening tests: a review with examples. Inhal Toxicol, 26(13): 811–828.

Mayo Clinic. (2020, March 19). Mayo Clinic. Retrieved from Preeclampsia: https://www.mayoclinic.org/diseases-conditions/preeclampsia/symptoms-causes/syc-20355745

MDCalc. (2020, November 20). MDCalc. Retrieved from CHA2DS2-VASc Score for Atrial Fibrillation Stroke Risk: https://www.mdcalc.com/cha2ds2-vasc-score-atrial-fibrillation-stroke-risk

Medcitynews. (2018, September 05). Medcitynews. Retrieved from FDA launches pilot payer program to help mitigate coverage woes for medtech startups: https://medcitynews.com/2018/09/fda-launches-pilot-payer-program-to-help-mitigate-coverage-woes-for-medtech-startups/

Medcitynews. (2019, November 14). Medcitynews. Retrieved from Omada Health lands first payer to deploy its Type 2 diabetes solution: https://medcitynews.com/2019/11/omada-health-lands-first-payer-to-deploy-its-type-2-diabetes-solution/

Medline Plus. (2020, November 19). Medline Plus. Retrieved from What is noninvasive prenatal testing (NIPT) and what disorders can it screen for?: https://medlineplus.gov/genetics/understanding/testing/nipt/#:~:text=Noninvasive%20prenatal%20testing%20(NIPT)%2C,in%20a%20pregnant%20woman's%20blood

Medline Plus. (2020, December 1). Medline Plus. Retrieved from C-Reactive Protein (CRP) Test: https://medlineplus.gov/lab-tests/c-reactive-protein-crp-test/

Medtek Norway. (2017). Health Technology Assessment in the Nordic Countries. Oslo: Medtek Norway.

Mihailovic, N. (2016). Review of Diagnosis-Related Group-Based Financing of Hospital Care. Health Services Research and Managerial Epidemiology, 1-8.

Ministere des Solidarites et de la Sante. (2020, November 27). Ministere des Solidarites et de la Sante. Retrieved from RIHN: https://solidarites-sante.gouv.fr/systeme-de-sante-et-medico-social/recherche-et-innovation/rihn#:~:text=de%20soins%20num%C3%A9riques%22-,Le%20r%C3%A9f%C3%A9rentiel%20des%20actes%20innovants%20hors%20nomenclature,et%20d'anatomopathologie%20(RIHN)&text=Ell

Ministère des solidarités et de la santé. (2020, April 9). Ministère des solidarités et de la santé. Retrieved from Le référentiel des actes innovants hors nomenclature de biologie et d'anatomopathologie (RIHN): https://solidarites-sante.gouv.fr/systeme-de-sante-et-medico-social/recherche-et-innovation/rihn

Ministère des Solidarités et de la Santé. (2020, November 27). Ministère des Solidarités et de la Santé. Retrieved from ÉTAPES : Expérimentations de Télémédecine pour l'Amélioration des Parcours En Santé: https://solidarites-sante.gouv.fr/soins-et-maladies/prises-en-charge-specialisees/telemedecine/article/etapes-experimentations-de-telemedecine-pour-l-amelioration-des-parcours-en

Ministero della Salute. (2020, November 26). Ministero della Salute. Retrieved from Nomenclatore dell'assistenza specialistica ambulatoriale: http://www.salute.gov.it/portale/lea/

dettaglioContenutiLea.jsp?
in-
gua=italiano&id=4701&area=Lea&menu=distrettuale

mySugr. (2018, July 16). mySugr. Retrieved from mySugr
secures competitive advantage by signing one of the
largest public health insurance companies in Germany: https://assets.mysugr.com/website/mysugr.com-
wordpress/uploads/2018/07/201807-mySugr-AOK-
Bayern-EN.pdf

mySugr. (2020, December 4). mySugr. Retrieved from
mySugr: https://www.mysugr.com/en/

National Cancer Institute. (2020, November 19). Cancer
terms. Retrieved from Definition liquid biopsy:
https://www.cancer.gov/publications/dictionaries/
cancer-terms/def/liquid-biopsy

Nesline, M. K. (2019). Oncologist uptake of comprehensive genomic profile guided targeted therapy. Oncotar-
get, 10(45): 4616–4629.

NHS England. (2020, November 27). NHS England. Retrieved from National Genomic Test Directories:
https://www.england.nhs.uk/publication/national-
genomic-test-directories/

NICE. (2016, May 11). PlGF-based testing to help diagnose suspected pre-eclampsia (Triage PlGF test, Elecsys immunoassay sFlt-1/PlGF ratio, DELFIA Xpress
PlGF 1-2-3 test, and BRAHMS sFlt-1 Kryptor/
BRAHMS PlGF plus Kryptor PE ratio). Retrieved from
PlGF-based testing to help diagnose suspected preeclampsia (Triage PlGF test, Elecsys immunoassay sFlt
-1/PlGF ratio, DELFIA Xpress PlGF 1-2-3 test, and

BRAHMS sFlt-1 Kryptor/BRAHMS PlGF plus Kryptor PE ratio): https://www.nice.org.uk/guidance/dg23

NICE. (2020, November 27). NICE. Retrieved from DAP: https://www.nice.org.uk/about/what-we-do/our-programmes/nice-guidance/nice-diagnostics-guidance

NICE. (2020, December 1). NICE DAP. Retrieved from NICE DAP: https://www.nice.org.uk/Media/Default/About/what-we-do/NICE-guidance/NICE-diagnostics-guidance/Diagnostics-assessment-programme-manual.pdf

OECD. (2020, November 26). OECD. Retrieved from Summary on Private health insurance in OECD countries: https://www.oecd.org/finance/insurance/1902544.pdf

Omada. (2020, December 4). Omada. Retrieved from Omada: https://www.omadahealth.com/

Oosterhoff, M. (2016). A Systematic Review of Health Economic Evaluations of Diagnostic Biomarkers. Appl Health Econ Health Policy, 51–65.

pharmacist.com. (2013, March 19). pharmacist.com. Retrieved from CMS cuts reimbursement for diabetes test supplies: https://www.pharmacist.com/cms-cuts-reimbursement-diabetes-test-supplies

PKV. (2020, November 26). PKV. Retrieved from PKV: https://www.pkv.de/service/rechtsquellen/gesetze-und-verordnungen/gebuehrenordnung-fuer-aerzte-goae.pdf

Proteinatlas. (2020, November 23). Proteinatlas. Retrieved from Immunohistochemistry: https://www.proteinatlas.org/learn/method/immunohistochemistry

Quest Diagnostics. (2014, October). 70% of medical decisions are based on lab results. Retrieved from https://
www.questdiagnostics.com/: https://
www.questdiagnostics.com/dms/Documents/
PLS/35841-FIN-WP-Hospital_Lab_Management-
WP4289.pdf

Rathenberg, J. (2014). Systematik der korrekten La-
borabrechnung – rechtliche Rahmenbedingungen. J
Lab Med, 179–205.

Rector, T. S. (2012). Methods Guide for Medical Test Re-
views. In T. S. Rector, Systematic Review of Prognostic
Tests (pp. 12-1 / 12-13). Rockville: Agency for
Healthcare Research and Quality.

Regione del Veneto. (2020, November 26). Bollettino Ufficiale della Regione del Veneto. Retrieved from Bollettino Ufficiale della Regione del Veneto: https://
bur.regione.veneto.it/BurvServices/Pubblica/
Download.aspx?
name=917_AllegatoA_188483.pdf&type=9&storico=F
alse

Roche. (2020, November 24). Roche. Retrieved from Co-
bas: https://diagnostics.roche.com/global/en/
products/systems/cobas_-6000-analyzer-series.html

Roche. (2020, November 24). Roche. Retrieved from Accu-
chek inform: https://diagnostics.roche.com/global/
en/products/instruments/accu-chek-inform-ii.html

Roche. (2020, November 20). Roche. Retrieved from El-
ecsys® sFlt-1/PlGF (Preeclampsia): https://
diagnostics.roche.com/global/en/products/params/
elecsys-sflt-1-plgf-preeclampsia.html

Rodger, M. (2012). Diagnostic randomized controlled trials: the final frontier. Trials, 13:137.

ScienceDirect. (2020, November 23). ScienceDirect. Retrieved from ELISA: https://www.sciencedirect.com/topics/immunology-and-microbiology/elisa

ScienceDirect. (2020, November 23). ScienceDirect. Retrieved from real time PCR: https://www.sciencedirect.com/topics/agricultural-and-biological-sciences/real-time-polymerase-chain-reaction

ScienceDirect. (2020, November 23). ScienceDirect. Retrieved from Next-generation-sequencing: https://www.sciencedirect.com/topics/nursing-and-health-professions/next-generation-sequencing

ScienceDirect. (2020, November 29). ScienceDirect. Retrieved from Mass spectroscopy: https://www.sciencedirect.com/topics/physics-and-astronomy/mass-spectroscopy

Sciencedirect. (2020, November 23). Sciencedirect. Retrieved from Fluorescence-in-situ-hybridization: https://www.sciencedirect.com/topics/biochemistry-genetics-and-molecular-biology/fluorescence-in-situ-hybridization

Shaw, J. L. (2016). Practical challenges related to point of care testing. Practical Laboratory Medicine, 22-29.

Siemens Healthineers. (2020, November 19). Siemens Healthineers. Retrieved from Cardiac Troponin: https://www.siemens-healthineers.com/laboratory-diagnostics/assays-by-diseases-conditions/cardiac-assays/cardiac-troponin-assays

Siemens Healthineers. (2020, November 24). Siemens Healthineers. Retrieved from Atellica: https://www.siemens-healthineers.com/integrated-chemistry/systems/atellica-solution-analyzers

SRF. (2020, June 25). SRF. Retrieved from Die Chancen für Tardoc stehen gut: https://www.srf.ch/news/schweiz/tarmed-nachfolge-aufgegleist-die-chancen-fuer-tardoc-stehen-gut

Tarmed Browser. (2020, December 08). Tarmed Browser. Retrieved from Tarmed Browser: https://www.tarmed-browser.ch/de

Taylor, C. (2010). Diagnosing Heart Failure – Experience And 'Best Pathways'. European Cardiology, 6(3):10–2.

TUV Sud. (2020, November 19). TUV Sud. Retrieved from Faq: In vitro diagnosti medical device regulation (IVDR): https://www.tuvsud.com/en/industries/healthcare-and-medical-devices/medical-devices-and-ivd/medical-device-market-approval-and-certification/eu-in-vitro-diagnostic-medical-device-regulation/faqs-in-vitro-diagnostic-medical-device-regulation-ivdr

University of Leads. (2020, November 23). University of Leads. Retrieved from What is histology: https://histology.leeds.ac.uk/what-is-histology/H_and_E.php

Viollier. (2018, June 1). Le vigaro. Retrieved from Humane Papillomaviren (HPV) Individuelle Risiken der High Risk-Typen: https://www.viollier.ch/sites/default/files/documents/levigaro/2018-07/lev_d_244_hpv_update.pdf

Voluntis. (2018, May 01). Voluntis. Retrieved from Investor Presentation: http://www.voluntis.com/files/investors/documents_a_telecharger/voluntis_investor_slideshow_20180514.pdf

WebMD. (2021, January 7). WebMD. Retrieved from WebMD: https://www.webmd.com/diabetes/guide/glycated-hemoglobin-test-hba1c

WHO. (2017). Guidance for procurement of in vitro diagnostics and related laboratory items and equipment. Geneva: WHO. Retrieved from Guidance for procurement of in vitro diagnostics and related laboratory items and equipment.

WHO. (2020, November 19). WHO. Retrieved from Health Technology Assessment: https://www.who.int/medical_devices/assessment/en/

ABOUT NORBERT FARKAS

Norbert Farkas is a Swiss-Hungarian citizen. He is the founder and managing partner of Centivis AG, a boutique (digital) diagnostics market access and policy consulting firm, based out of Switzerland.

Prior to starting his own advisory firm, he supported multiple innovative pharmaceuticals, vaccines and in-vitro diagnostics product launches from the access and policy perspectives at Novartis and Roche global headquarters. He started his career at the European Parliament. Norbert holds a Master's Degree in Economics from the Budapest University of Economics and Public Administration and an MBA from University of St. Gallen.

He regularly coaches digital health start-ups and lectures health policy students at University of Lucerne.

Connect with Norbert at:

Linkedin.com/in/norbertfarkas

NOTES

WANT TO LEARN MORE?

If after reading this book, you would like to learn more about topics we discussed, please visit our frequently updated blog section:

Centivis.com/news

You can download free reports on diagnostics reimbursement pathways, country periodic tariff changes and diagnostic test reports:

Centivis.com/insights

Or just simply sign up to the mailing list to receive our monthly newsletter delivered in your inbox:

Centivis.com